THE
REAL MADRID
HANDBOOK

A CONCISE HISTORY OF REAL MADRID

RAB MACWILLIAM

This edition first published in 2022 by

POLARIS PUBLISHING LTD
c/o Aberdein Considine
2nd Floor, Elder House
Multrees Walk
Edinburgh, EH1 3DX

Distributed by
Birlinn Limited

www.polarispublishing.com

ISBN: 9781913538828
eBook ISBN: 9781913538835

THIS IS AN UNOFFICIAL PRODUCT

British Library Cataloguing-in-Publication Data
A catalogue record for this book is available on request from the British Library.

Designed and typeset by Polaris Publishing, Edinburgh
Printed in Great Britain by MBM Print SCS Limited, East Kilbride

INTRODUCTION

'Spain is the problem, and Europe is the solution.'
José Ortega y Gasset

'Real Madrid is the most important thing that happened to me,
both as a footballer and as a person.'
Zinedine Zidane

'Spain is different'

Although rough-and-ready versions of the game had for centuries
been enjoyed across the world, football – as we know it today –
was first codified and developed in England during the second
half of the 19th century.

The game quickly spread across the world, and it was introduced
to other countries by sailors, travellers, workmen and students. In
Europe, today's leading footballing nations were eager enthusiasts
for the game and were establishing football clubs by the early
years of the 20th century. However, out of all the major European
countries which have embraced this most appealing of games, the
story of football in Spain is the most complex and remarkable.

In Spain, one must consider football – as with many aspects of
Spanish culture – within the context of the country's historically

divisive, frequently contradictory and singularly confusing history. It is one which has, over the centuries, permeated and shaped all aspects of Spanish life in ways with which few European countries can identify.

Only 70 or so years ago, the country was regarded as a pariah state: an authoritarian regime, internally disputatious, perilously close to bankruptcy, and internationally tolerated but widely ignored. Today, Spain is a prosperous and unitary country, a member of the EU, and recognised globally as a nation equal in status to all other European countries. Spain's complex history has been mirrored by its arrival in the highest echelons of world club football, and few clubs have been as internationally influential and dominant in the game as have Real Madrid.

In the book I cover the story of the club – from the early 20th century years, through their progress in the domestic cup and league, the Republic, the Spanish Civil War and its repressive authoritarian aftermath. I then relate how the stunning success in European football competition of the exceptional Real Madrid side of the mid-1950s to the early 1960s was one of the factors which helped to ease Spain's integration into Europe.

Although the development of mass tourism, and its associated socio-economic liberalisation, led to the gradual decline of Francoism and the stigma of the bloody Spanish Civil War, the growing awareness of the country's footballing talents – in particular, those of Real Madrid – generated a wide appeal across the continent and contributed to the change in the perception of Spain and its acceptance into the wider world. Since then, Real Madrid have been, and today remain, at the forefront of Spanish football's rise to prominence as one of the most skilful and dominant countries in the European – and, indeed, in the global – game.

Over the following pages I offer a necessarily brief but, I hope, informative and entertaining account of the club's origins and development, the games, players, incidents, personalities and much else which have contributed to Real Madrid's contemporary status as one of the world's leading and best-supported football clubs.

I hope you enjoy reading it.

Rab MacWilliam
July 2022

Why Madrid?

Throughout its 'Golden Age' in the 16th and most of the 17th century, Spain was one of the most powerful countries in Europe and far beyond. The country's rise to dominance had been achieved mainly by its twin policies of extensive colonisation, particularly in Latin America, and formidable naval strength.

Internally, however, the country was an unco-ordinated, fragmented, frequently mutually hostile and constantly suspicious assembly of small kingdoms and regions. In the eyes of its rulers, it required firm control. When one of these rulers, the Holy Roman Emperor Charles V, abdicated in the mid-16th century, his son Philip II became King of Spain.

In 1561, Philip moved his court to the small town of Madrid, with its population of under 20,000, which was in Castile and which he then declared to be the capital of Spain. Until that point, other than its 600–1,000m-high *meseta* (the Castilian Central Plateau) having served as a useful lookout point between the Christian North and the Islamic South, this settlement, surrounded by forests and mountain ranges, possessed no obvious qualifications for such a role. It also lacked a harbour, its river the Manzanares saw few passing boats, and its temperature varied between freezing in winter and relentless summer heat.

However, for Philip II, Madrid had the overriding benefit of its location in the centre of Spain. By selecting Madrid as the home of his court and, therefore, as the capital of the country, he was attempting to show no favour to particular areas and to ensure the equal status of all the troublesome regions within Spain.

From now on, Spain was to be controlled from and by Madrid.

Madrid in the 21st century

Today, almost 500 years later, Madrid has a population of around 7 million people and is a very different place from that small, unobtrusive settlement. The city has become Spain's most densely populated region, and it is the country's economic, financial and diplomatic centre. Much has happened over the years in this quarrelsome country, but Madrid remains, as it was in Philip's vision, the heart and capital city of Spain.

There is much that can be, and has been, written about the city's history but, this being a football book, I will restrict myself to the game. The 20th century gave birth to a number of football clubs in Madrid, and several have stood the test of time and continued, since their inception, in various divisions in the national league.

These include Rayo Majadahonda, Alcorcón, Leganés, Getafe, Rayo Vallecano and the city's 'second' club Atlético Madrid. In recent years, in particular, Atlético, under Diego Simeone, have again become a leading national club; Getafe, Leganés and Rayo Vallecano have tended to follow the *equipo ascenseur* ('elevator team' or 'yo-yo' club) model; and the first two seem content with their lower-division status.

However, there is one other club in the city whose origins, history and international fame eclipse all others in the capital, in the country and in European football generally. That club is, of course, Real Madrid.

3

'Los Blancos'

Known to millions of fans as 'Los Merengues', 'Los Blancos', 'Los Vikingos', 'La Casa Blanca' and similar friendly nicknames, but referred to by supporters of rival clubs in rather less affectionate terms, Real Madrid are nonetheless the best-known and most successful club in world football.

(In this book, I refer throughout to the club as 'Real', unless this creates ambiguity, which is when I use the full name. I also refer to them and other clubs in the plural, as this is a conversational convention and recognises that clubs are a collection of many players and other members.)

Since they were formed 120 years ago, Real have won their national league a record 35 times and claimed Spain's national cup on 19 occasions. In the European Cup/Champions League they can boast an unequalled 14 trophies, as well as numerous other European and global awards. In the year 2000, Real Madrid were honoured by FIFA – the organisation which governs world football – as the 'Club of the 20th Century'.

But what were the origins of this footballing giant?

Real kick off

The first football club to be formally established in the city of Madrid was called, unsurprisingly, the Madrid Football Club.

In 1897, a team calling itself Sociedad Sky Football, usually known as 'La Sociedad', began to play on Sundays in the city. Sky were the sporting outlet for a new organisation – the Institución Libre de Enseñanza (Free Institute of Learning) – which had been formed as a liberal, secular and pro-Enlightenment counterpoint to the conservative views and strict Catholic orthodoxy which until then had dominated Spanish life and culture.

The Sociedad Sky captain was a 23-year-old British businessman, Arthur Johnson, who believed that football could be a positive force in challenging the deeply entrenched, class-ridden system which had for centuries enchained so much of the country. Johnson was also an enthusiastic, knowledgeable football trainer, an exceptionally good player and a pleasant fellow, all of which helped to cement his reputation as 'un Inglés muy simpático'.

In 1900, several members left Sky to set up a new club, Nuevo Sociedad de Football, which was in 1901 renamed Madrid Football Club and was under the direction of one Julián Palacios. Palacios is claimed by Real as their first president, but Nuevo Sociedad were then still an informal gathering of football enthusiasts rather than a legally organised institution.

Other dissidents who joined Madrid FC included brothers Juan and Carlos Padrós, who were born in Barcelona but had moved to the capital as children. They ran a clothes shop, located a few hundred yards to the south of today's Santiago Bernabéu Stadium. Their Catalonian connection, however, is curiously absent from the Real official records. After a 1902 restructuring – and to complicate matters further – Sky also changed their name to New Foot Ball Club.

Eventually, in the late afternoon of Thursday 6 March 1902, a meeting was held in a back room of the clothing shop. The company was established as a legally constituted entity, a board of directors was elected, and Juan Padrós became the first formal president of Madrid FC, the forerunner of Real.

The Real Madrid team in 1902. *Alamy*

Coronation Cup of 1902

Such was the mass appeal of the new sport of football that, by the early 20th century, other clubs were already being established across the country.

The first official club was Recreativo de Huelva ('El Decano' or 'The Dean'), instituted in 1889 by employees of the Rio Tinto British mining community in Andalucia. In 1898, FC Barcelona arrived on the scene, closely followed by Athletic Club Bilbao in 1901. With the advent of Madrid FC the following year, what were to become known as the 'Big Three' Spanish clubs – Athletic Bilbao, Barcelona and Real (at that time Madrid FC) – were eagerly awaiting Spain's first official football tournament.

This national competition took place on 13/14 May 1902 at the Madrid Hippodrome, only a couple of months after Madrid FC's formation. Held to commemorate the coronation of King Alfonso XIII, it was named the Coronation Cup. However, from the following year it became Spain's first annual national football competition, the Copa del Rey (King's Cup), until the arrival of La Liga in 1929. The Copa del Rey today remains the national annual knockout competition in Spain.

The Coronation Cup was the first opportunity for these new clubs to test themselves in competition against other clubs and regions. Five clubs turned up: Madrid FC, Foot Ball Club Barcelona, Club Español de Foot Ball (another Catalan team),

Vizcaya (mainly Athletic Bilbao plus a few other Basque players) and New Foot Ball Club.

The Cup also witnessed the first game between Barcelona and Madrid FC, a confrontation which was to become known as 'El Clásico'. Barcelona, a more experienced side, won 3-1, with Arthur Johnson's goal for Madrid FC ensuring that a British player scored Real Madrid's first-ever official goal. The competition was won by a strong Vizcaya team who beat Barcelona 2-1 in the final.

The Cup was regarded by spectators and players alike as a successful venture. Extra wooden stands had to be installed in the Hippodrome to accommodate the larger-than-expected crowds, while the quality of the football was impressive. Madrid FC had shown they could hold their own against other top regional clubs, and bullfighting now faced a growing challenge to its historical role as the most popular Spanish 'spectator sport'.

'Real Madrid': the early years

From their 1902 beginning until the present day, Madrid FC, or Real (Royal) Madrid as they were formally renamed by Alfonso XIII in 1920, have played in an all-white strip, which was modelled on the white strip worn by England's first successful club, Corinthians. The plain strips were also cheaper than the artificially dyed variety: the president of the club was, after all, a clothier.

In 1903, another new club was formed in the city but, unlike some smaller teams, which were by now disappearing, this one was to prove an enduring rival to Madrid FC. Three Basque students, with the assistance of footballing friends and a few ex-members of Madrid FC, set up Athletic Madrid – which would become Atlético Madrid – and adopted Athletic Bilbao as their 'parent club'. They played in the Basque club's colours until the dissolution of their relationship almost 20 years later.

The first Copa del Rey competition kicked off in 1903, with only Español and Athletic Bilbao as competitors to Madrid FC. Athletic Bilbao beat Madrid to win the competition, which was watched by a crowd of 5,000, and Athletic repeated the feat in 1904. Between 1905 and 1908, however, Madrid returned the compliment by winning the Copa four times in succession, with Athletic Bilbao being the losing finalist on each occasion. Thereafter, Madrid did not win the Copa again until 1917.

The 1906 team, who won the club's second Copa del Rey. *Alamy*

In common with the many other football clubs which were now appearing across Spain, Madrid FC competed in local and regional leagues, played friendly matches against local sides and regularly entered the national Copa del Rey.

By 1910, Andalucia had Sevilla (1905) and Betis (1907); in the Basque Country were Real Sociedad (1909) and Arenas de Getxo (1909); Galicia's Deportivo de La Coruña saw the light of day in 1906, just three years before Valencia's Levante (1909); the oldest club in Catalonia was Palamós (1896); and there were a good many others in existence or under consideration in the various regions of the country. The need for a national league system was becoming increasingly apparent.

Grounds for change

In 1910, Madrid FC was one of the founder members of the Royal Spanish Football Federation (RSFF), a national organisation charged with running the Spanish game and which continues in this role today. But it was to be almost another 20 years before the national league came into being.

Meanwhile, in 1912, Madrid FC moved to a new stadium, Campo de O'Donnell, which was the club's first purpose-built ground and had its own small wooden stand. The ground was named in honour of Leopoldo O'Donnell, a mid-19th-century military man and influential politician. Prior to this, the team had played on grassy fields in the city and had no place of their own.

As a sign of the confidence they placed in the club, the Madrid FC socios (members) funded the new ground. Madrid inaugurated the stadium on 31 October 1912 with a game against one of the leading Basque clubs, Sporting de Irún (later Real Unión). The resulting 0-0 draw was a highly creditable result for Madrid.

In 1920, when Alfonso XIII bestowed on Madrid the title of 'Real', they were not the first Spanish team to receive this honour, but their membership – impressed by this regal association – increased significantly. Although the 1920s were for Real a period of 'development' in which they won little of significance, their membership outgrew the confines of the O'Donnell ground and they moved to a larger stadium.

First, they played in a velodrome in Ciudad Lineal in the north-east of the city. Although its capacity was 8,000, it proved too far away for many of their fans, and Real remained there for only one year. They then moved back to the north of Madrid and built the Chamartin (close to today's Bernabéu) with room for 15,000 spectators.

To inaugurate this new stadium – which would be their home for the next 22 years – Real invited English FA Cup holders Newcastle United to play them in the opening game. Real inflicted a 3-2 defeat on the Geordies, a side highly regarded in the homeland of football. Despite the absence of trophies, Real were already demonstrating the growing quality of the Spanish club game.

The Campo de Chamartin. *stadiumguide.com*

Regional rivalries

However, as the standard of football had been rising across the country, so too had regional rivalries. This was particularly the case in those regions which had long considered themselves 'different', especially Catalonia and the Basque Country. Madrid, as the capital, was perceived by many inhabitants of these lands as the centralised essence and bastion of all things 'Spanish'.

To a degree, the game of football in most countries is driven by and, in turn, stimulates similar rivalries and encounters. Spain, however, has throughout its history been a shifting confederation of frequently competing cities and states, several with their own language and culture, and their inter-regional hostilities were and are significantly more marked than elsewhere in the European game.

There are early footballing examples which reveal this centralist–regional distrust. For instance, as the Copa del Rey expanded its scope, the enmity and on-pitch violence involving certain areas in the peninsula became apparent, with FC Barcelona and Athletic Bilbao being the most vociferous exponents.

When Real reached the Copa final in 1916 (and were beaten 4-0 by Athletic Bilbao), they had replayed Barcelona four times in the semi-final, with each encounter being more bruising and creating more mutual antipathy than the last. Madrid reached the final after the Barcelona captain led his team off the pitch, citing referee bias. In the following year's Copa final – a 2-1 Madrid defeat of Basque club Arenas de Getxo – the semi-final against Catalonia's Español was again marred by pitch invasions and violence.

Campo de O'Donnell in Madrid hosted the Madrid–Barcelona Copa match in 1916. *Marca*

The 1920 Olympics

One major international event which did, however, unite the disparate footballing regions of Spain was the Olympic Games, held in Antwerp in 1920.

Spain were invited to compete in the Games, and the country saw this as an opportunity to emerge from the relative wilderness and gain the international respect it felt it deserved. Spain sent its first football squad, 21 players all from the north of the country as that was their home, under the management of Paco Bru. The game's Spanish luminaries – including Zamora and Samitier from Barcelona and 'Pichichi' from Athletic Bilbao – all played in what proved to be a chaotic football tournament.

However, they defeated Sweden, Italy and the Netherlands to claim the silver medal – Belgium won the gold – and give birth to the term *La Furia Española* (the Spanish fury). Winning the silver medal generated, albeit briefly, a sense of pride and a feeling of belonging to an all-encompassing Spanish footballing nation. This was one of the major factors behind the game's rapid increase in popularity across the country, even in those central and southerly regions such as Madrid which had been virtually ignored by the Spanish football selectors.

In the short term, every football club in Spain benefited from this sentiment, although the aggressive nationalism implicit in La Furia Española gradually became associated with the right-wing Falange party and its Francoist supporters.

Planning for a league

The post-Olympic surge in the extent and intensity of loyalty to Spanish football clubs was accompanied by an increasing commercialisation and professionalisation of the game. By the mid-1920s, Real, with their well-off, bourgeois membership's financial backing, were luring and signing top players from other Spanish clubs, generally to the irritation of the less wealthy ones.

Real had also been developing a youth system (*cantera*) and fielding their own players, such as inside-forward Santiago Bernabéu, a name which will increasingly recur later in this book as he became the most influential and dominant individual in the club's history. They had learnt much from their overseas tours, including several games in England in 1925, a three-month tour of Latin America in 1927 (organised by Bernabéu, now retired from playing and having become the club's general manager) and several 'friendlies' against European sides.

Real were now ready to challenge similarly ambitious and expansive Spanish clubs in regular competition. The Copa del Rey had until then been the only national measure of clubs' ranking, but, as with all knockout competitions, it could be a fickle and often freakish barometer. What was required was a national league containing clubs of a similar footballing standard playing on a home-and-away basis with matches held annually over an agreed number of months.

Santiago Bernabéu, playing at Campo de O'Donnell. *Marca*

La Liga begins

After many debates and much double-talk, and after all the trouble and the strife, the interested parties agreed on the structure of the new league, to be called La Liga.

La Liga was to consist of two divisions – Primera and Segunda – each containing ten clubs. The Primera, or top division, comprised the six winners of the Copa (originally Arenas de Getxo, Athletic de Bilbao, Barcelona, Real Madrid, Real Sociedad, Real Unión), the three most frequent runners-up (Athletic de Madrid, Español, Europa), with the tenth slot decided by knockout (in this case, Rácing de Santander, who defeated Sevilla).

Segunda began with eight clubs which today are some of Spain's best-known names (Sevilla, Alavés, Sporting de Gijón, Valencia, Real Betis, Real Oviedo, Deportivo de La Coruña, Celta Vigo) and two which have dropped from sight (Iberia and Rácing de Madrid). Promotion and relegation were to be decided by a play-off between the bottom club in Primera and the winner of Segunda. The season was originally to begin in early February and conclude in late June, and all games were to be played both home and away.

Compared to the complexity of today's Liga (twice as many clubs in Primera, the emergence of Segunda B and Tercera with 440 clubs in these lower two tiers, the competition with European tournaments, and so on), the establishment of the tournament appeared straightforward. However, this being Spain, and with a land mass twice the size of the UK, it proved tricky to administer, but it seemed to work. The organisation of La Liga was aided by the determination of the larger clubs to win the title, and the improvement in the 1920s of the national railway system under the brief, authoritarian rule of Primo de Rivera.

La Liga expands

In the early years of La Liga, one of the important reasons for its smooth running was that nine of the original ten Primera teams were from three nearby regions – Catalonia, Castile and the Basque Country – with the tenth club, Santander, based in Cantabria, just up the road. This made travel and accommodation easier and quicker and, anyway, most of these clubs knew each other rather well. As La Liga expanded, however, its reach began to include clubs in regions with which many of the original players and supporters were unfamiliar.

Within five years of its establishment, for instance, Primera embraced such clubs as Valencia, Oviedo and Real Betis. Two years later, in season 1935/36, and now enlarged to 12 clubs, Primera hosted Hércules, Osasuna, Sevilla and Athletic de Madrid. Madrid (or Madrid FC, which it again became after the establishment of the Second Republic and the abdication of Alfonso XIII in 1931), Barcelona, Athletic Bilbao and Español were the only clubs that season which remained from 1929. Indeed, Real, Athletic Bilbao and Barcelona are, to this day, the only clubs never to have been relegated from Primera.

The discovery of these regions – often with their own dialect or language, culture and political views – must have raised questions in the minds of their footballing visitors. Most of them had never before left their own *pueblo* areas or encountered Spain's diversity, complexity and fragility. Arriving at the time they did, the cross-country insights revealed by La Liga's expansion may have been a factor – although clearly not a major one – in the impending and horrifying Spanish Civil War.

Real Madrid in La Liga

Real kicked off their first game in Primera on 10 February 1929, shortly after their defeat by Español in the Copa final and Bernabéu's election to the club's board. Four goals from Jaime Lazcano, signed by Bernabéu from Osasuna, helped Real in their 5-0 win over Europa at Chamartin. Then they beat Barcelona and, in the inaugural Derbi Madrileño, the first of over 220 such matches, they defeated city neighbours Athletic de Madrid. Real had a successful season in 1929, and the title was decided in the final matches, when Real lost, Barcelona won, and the Catalan club claimed the first Liga title.

The following season (1929/30) was disappointing, with Real gaining a solitary point from their first five games, and even their 6-0 hammering of Santander hardly improved matters as they ended in fifth place, 13 points behind Athletic Bilbao. The Basque club was the dominant team of the pre-Civil War era. Coached by Englishman Fred Pentland, their style of football was based on the British game, with its emphasis on passing and interchange of positions rather than the traditional Spanish long-ball game, and it worked well for Bilbao as they secured the *doblete* (double) that season by also winning the Copa.

Before the 1930/31 season got under way, Real reached the final of the Copa, and they faced Athletic Bilbao at 'neutral' Español's Montjuic Stadium in Barcelona. The Basques and

Catalans enjoyed, on the surface at least, a mutual sympathy and an unwritten pact against what they increasingly perceived as the imperious centralism of Real Madrid. This was made clear before the game even kicked off, when the largely Catalan crowd cheered Bilbao onto the pitch but loudly jeered Real Madrid's entrance.

This cacophony of hostility continued whenever Real had the ball. With ten minutes remaining and the score 2-2, Real scored a seemingly legitimate goal but, for reasons of his own, the Catalan referee disallowed it. In extra time, Bilbao scored what proved to be the winner and claimed the trophy. As the Real players left the pitch, several of them were pushed and jostled by the crowd, and a confused and disheartened Real Madrid left town with all possible haste.

Madrid's newspapers accused the Basque and Catalan supporters of rabid victimisation and, although outrage sells newspapers, in this case they had a point. But the regional enmity simply increased in intensity over the coming years.

'It's Zamora'

In 1930, Bernabéu acquired the acclaimed Español keeper Ricardo Zamora. Regarded as Spain's finest goalkeeper, he had been the 19-year-old custodian for the 1920 Spanish Olympic team and was later memorably described as 'more famous than Garbo, and better-looking'.

He was also a controversial character and celebrity, who was named 'Best Goalkeeper' at the 1934 World Cup and whose name lives on today in the Zamora trophy, established by *Marca* football magazine in 1958 as an award given annually to La Liga's best goalie. Zamora was the first but by no means the last of Bernabéu's big-name signings. Injured on his debut match, Zamora was out of action for eight games, and his return was too late to save Real's 1930/31 season as they finished in sixth place.

Before the following season, Bernabéu again displayed his wily intelligence, and his access to considerable funding, by persuading defenders Jacinto Quincoces and Errasti Ciriaco to leave Alavés and join Real. Quincoces, especially, proved himself one of the finest defenders in the club's history. He was voted 'Best Defender' in the 1934 World Cup and was the club manager in the 1940s. Although neither of these players came cheaply, Real Madrid (or Madrid FC as they were renamed under the new Republican government) had a wealthy socio hinterland and an ambitious Bernabéu. With Zamora's skilfully intimidating presence on the

24

goal line, the team could now boast La Liga's toughest and most goal-proof defence.

. . . and the 'Lobster Man'

In season 1931/32, Madrid FC walked away with La Liga title, their first trophy since 1917, remaining undefeated throughout, winning ten and drawing eight games and conceding only 15 goals.

The following season, 1932/33, they retained the title, partly because of another sizeable splash-out from Bernabéu. He snatched Josep Samitier – the first Spanish player to perfect the 'midfield general' role and who had travelled with Zamora to the 1920 Olympics – from his long-term club Barcelona.

A 'bon viveur' and friend of Zamora, Samitier was a man of similarly dubious celebrity. His ball control, trickery and mastery of the 'bicycle kick' had earned him the curious nickname of 'the Lobster Man'. At the age of 31, his tactical awareness and passing talent remained impeccable. Shortly after his arrival at Madrid, he scored both goals in their 2-1 home win over his former club, and, to rub it in, Madrid FC ended that season as Liga winners, an emphatic nine points ahead of Barcelona.

For the next two seasons, Madrid FC managed only second place in La Liga: first, behind Real Betis's solitary Liga title, and then trailing Athletic Bilbao, whose era-dominating period in Spanish football was nearing its conclusion.

'El Divino's' save

Walk into any bar near a football stadium in Spain. If they have photos on the wall, then it's a safe bet that there will be a black-and-white shot of a diving goalie wearing a bonnet, surrounded by a cloud of dust, with his left-hand post in the centre of the frame (see overleaf). The keeper, diving at full stretch to his left, is Ricardo Zamora, and he's just made the most famous save in Spanish footballing history.

This 'impossible save', as it's universally known, was made by Zamora – 'El Divino' – in the dying seconds of the first El Clásico final ever contested between Madrid FC (Real Madrid) and Barcelona. It took place at the last official game of the 1935/36 season – the final of the Copa del Presidente de la República (as the Copa del Rey had been retitled under the Republic) – which was played in Valencia's Mestalla Stadium on 21 June 1936. Despite playing with ten men for much of the match, Madrid were 2-1 ahead of the Catalans. In the final seconds, Barcelona's Josep Escola launched a screaming, goalbound shot from the edge of the box. Initially unsighted, Zamora made a superb save, emerging from the dust with a smile on his face and the ball safely clutched in his hands.

Moments later, Madrid FC had won the Copa, and El Divino was lifted up and carried around the pitch by delighted Madrid fans celebrating their seventh Copa title as well as memories of the greatest save that any of them had ever seen.

This was the last official game in Spanish national league and cup football for three years. Franco launched his Nationalist rebellion against the democratically elected Spanish Republic on 18 July 1936, and the Spanish Civil War began. Football continued at local and regional level, but soon there were considerably more important things to consider than kicking a ball about a pitch.

Football in the Civil War

No matter your subject of historical interest – whether it be coal mining in Cantabria or melon growing in Andalucia – it would be folly to ignore the impact on your specialist study of the Spanish Civil War, as it affected everyone. It would also be an insult to the 500,000 people killed during or as a result of this bloody, internecine conflict which raged across Spain for almost three years.

Oddly enough, given the game's mass popular base and therefore its potential for political manipulation, football was not too badly affected by the murderous mayhem which savaged other activities in the country. The game at the national level was badly disrupted, as some of the clubs (Sevilla, Deportivo de La Coruña) were in Nationalist areas while others (Valencia, Levante) were found in Republican ones. The latter were not susceptible to Nationalist interference, but elsewhere Francoists were in control.

However, Franco and his generals believed that the sport served the function of deflecting attention away from the atrocities being routinely carried out in the name of Spain. They thought that football was a useful distraction from the fiercely pro-Catholic, authoritarian and deeply anti-democratic onward march of the military and its Nationalist supporters.

Regional and local games were encouraged, mainly in the countryside. But many of the larger towns and cities remained

Republican and were too busy organising defences against Nationalist incursions, or arguing among themselves, to think about football.

Barcelona and Bilbao

Barcelona was badly affected by the war, but for most of the conflict the city was located well within the Republican area. However, despite the death of its president Josep Sunyol in 1936 near Madrid at the hands of Nationalist troops, Barcelona FC survived the internal political struggles and the attacks on the city.

In 1937, the club played in a Republican-approved Mediterranean League. They also travelled on an American tour which was financed by a Mexican banker and, when a residue of the players arrived back home, they had raised sufficient funds to save the club from imminent bankruptcy.

Bilbao, although much closer to the front line of the fighting, also remained a Republican city. Athletic Bilbao, however, in 1937 formed a squad of 20 Basque players, mainly from Athletic Club but also from such clubs as Real Betis, Athletic Madrid and others. Under the name Republik Euzkadi they were sent to Europe to publicise the Basque cause.

In Paris, the Euzkadi players were told about the devastation of the Basque spiritual home of Guernica and then, on a three-month tour of the USSR, they found out about the Francoist takeover of Bilbao. As a result, many of the team found themselves unable or unwilling to return home. The squad next moved to Latin America, in particular to Mexico, where several of them played regularly until the end of the Civil War.

Madrid in the Civil War

There remains a myth, propagated partly by some dissenting regions, that Madrid was a welcoming home to Francoists during the Civil War. The reality is that the capital was on the front line and under sustained Nationalist siege from virtually the beginning of the war until its bitter conclusion.

The city came under the de facto control of left-wing worker militias and communist factions, and it was Republican throughout the conflict. The Republican government, alarmed by the onslaught, had moved from Madrid to the relative safety of Valencia in 1936. Madrid's inhabitants suffered continual deaths from artillery and aircraft shelling, starvation and poverty. Although the Nationalists made incursions into Madrid's suburbs, the city's leaders would not submit to the Francoist forces. Despite some internal dissent and violence, they would not surrender, and Madrid increasingly became a Popular Front island in a virtual sea of Francoism.

Madrid FC's Chamartin stadium and pitch were used not, as has been alleged, for a Francoist prison camp, but for various activities, such as a parade ground, exercise space for workers' groups, political rallies and the storage of military equipment. The seating, brickwork and pitch were almost ruined, and the wooden stands were burnt for fuel. Unlike the numerous games played by Basques and Catalans, the club hardly played a single match during the Civil War.

Madrid, to the bitter end

Madrid FC's coach Paco Bru, who had managed Spain to their silver medal in the 1920 Olympics, applied in October 1937 to the Catalan Republican authorities for his club to join the Mediterranean League. Although the smaller clubs in Catalonia, mindful of the economic and prestigious benefits of Madrid FC coming to town, happily supported this proposal, the application was turned down by Barcelona FC, the only regional club to do so.

Although posters had appeared in Barcelona saying 'Defensar Madrid és defensar Catalunya' (To defend Madrid is to defend Catalonia), and although there had been comradely pledges of friendship made by Barcelona to Madrid, Barcelona FC – probably through a combination of long-term rivalry and concern that their league dominance might be challenged – condemned Madrid FC to a long period of footballing inactivity.

When, in March 1939, Madrid – a city which had withstood Franco for longer than anywhere else in Spain – had no option but to surrender, the acting president of Madrid FC, Antonio Ortega, the communist colonel of a workers' militia, was executed. Strangely, Ortega receives no mention in Real's official history. The formal, longer-term president, Rafael Sánchez Guerra – a staunch Republican who had been offered a safe escape to Valencia by his comrades, but declined the offer – was eventually sentenced by Francoists to a long prison term.

The incoming Nationalist troops exacted a murderous revenge on many Madrileños. On 1 April 1939, Franco issued a communiqué: 'The War is over.' As Sid Lowe comments in his book *Fear and Loathing in La Liga*: 'Once Madrid fell, everything fell.'

The Plaza del Oriente in Madrid after the invasion of the Spanish troops under General Francisco Franco in the spring of 1939. In the background, the Spanish Royal Palace (Palacio Real). In front of it, the equestrian statue of King Philip IV (Felipe IV, 1605–1665). The pavement of the square is torn open for barricade construction. *Alamy*

The post-war years

The Spanish Civil War virtually destroyed Real Madrid (Franco permitted, in 1943, a return to their previous name). As well as a ruined Chamartin stadium, only a few of the pre-war team returned to the club or were in a fit state to play, the club had little money, and the membership had declined significantly in number. Real Madrid's footballing future was a precarious one.

Real's bleak position was compounded by the agreement of their city rivals Athletic Madrid to join with the new Francoist regime's air-force side in a team called Atlético Aviación and to play in La Liga. Not only did the merger permit concessions unavailable to other clubs but it also provided the club with access to some quality players. The club's new status was an ironic one, as Athletic had been formally relegated at the end of the 1935/36 season. However, after the war, Oviedo's ground was a shambles and, although Oviedo should have been promoted, Athletic stayed in Primera. The Atlético team was managed by ex-Real keeper Ricardo Zamora, a Nationalist supporter.

Despite their handicaps, and with volunteers helping to restore the Chamartin, the new-look Real played their first post-war match in December 1939. Although the club had to rebuild over the following few years, during which period they generally languished in La Liga, they finished in fourth position in Primera in 1939/40, the first post-war season. With hindsight, this appears a defiant but futile performance, as they ended 1940/41 in sixth place and manager Paco Bru was fired.

Again, Real demonstrated their potential the next season by finishing second in Primera, now extended to include 14 clubs. However, the opposition – in the shape of Barcelona, Athletic Bilbao and the temporarily resurgent Sevilla (the first city occupied by Franco) and Valencia – ensured Real's secondary status over these few years. In 1942/43, they sank to the bottom half of Primera, but somehow engineered an extraordinary result against Barcelona in the 1943 Copa semi-final.

Real Madrid 11 . . . Barcelona 1

The first leg of the 1943 Copa del Generalissimo semi-final took place at Barcelona's Les Corts ground, and the home team – winners the previous year – dominated the game, winning 3-0 against a subdued Real. The visitors, a lowly tenth in La Liga that season, were subjected to whistling and booing whenever they touched the ball and were constantly kicked and fouled by the Barcelona team. As a result of this blatant hostility, Barcelona were fined and their supporters banned from attending the second leg of the El Clásico in Madrid on 13 June.

How, then, did Real manage to beat Barcelona in the second leg by the staggering scoreline of 11 goals to one (yes, 11-1)? True, Barcelona were exposing themselves to 20,000 revenge-seeking Madridismos who were all armed with whistles, handed out by the club at the ground's entrances. True, for the Real players this was payback time for the physical assaults they had suffered at Les Corts. True, the two clubs were not, to put it mildly, close and affectionate comrades. And it is also true that unexpected results can occur in cup ties, although rarely to this extent.

But is it also true, as some authorities and commentators allege, that the Francoist Director of State Security visited the Barcelona players before kick-off and reminded them that it was only thanks to the generosity of Franco's regime that they and their families were still at liberty and, indeed, alive? Is it true that the Barcelona keeper hardly dared enter his own penalty area due to the offensive and potentially lethal objects which were illegally being hurled, without police interference, into his goalmouth? Or was the keeper, Luis Mort, paid by the Real management to let in the goals? Certainly, he never again played for Barcelona. Or did Barcelona, in the vernacular, just bottle it? The last two conjectures seem unlikely, but one never can tell, particularly in the atmosphere of must-win El Clásicos.

Whatever the reason behind the astonishing result, the game kicked off at the appointed time. After 45 minutes, the score was 8-0 to Real Madrid, and during the interval a few Barcelona players were so dispirited by the atmosphere that they wanted to forget about appearing for the second half and, instead, leg it home. Football, however, is a game which requires a resilient team spirit and a determination to defeat the odds, so they trotted out again onto the enemy pitch.

After 90 excruciating minutes, and an 11-1 defeat by Real's 'heroes' (as they are described in the club's official history), the Catalan contingent – humiliated and enraged in equal measure – boarded the team coach and sped homewards to the safety and sunlit plains of home.

Peace in our time

As a result of this game, the then president resigned from Real. In September 1943, Santiago Bernabéu was elected in his place, 30 years after joining the club where he would serve as a player, general manager and director. His election was to mark the beginning of a new era for the club.

Real's management seemed genuinely embarrassed by the 11-1 result and were also concerned at the increasing number of attacks from Barcelona and other clubs concerning their supposed Francoist connection. Bernabéu asked the government to issue a circular to newspapers which prohibited any mention of the result, and the Francoist authorities complied with his request.

Real suggested home-and-away *partidos de la paz* (peace matches) as 'compensation'. At the first such game at Chamartin, Barcelona were welcomed with live music, dancing, flowers and an ovation from the crowd, and the score was 1-1. At the second game at Les Corts, the pantomime was reversed, if not outdone in its fervent splendour. Barca won 4-0, and both sides were under orders to restrain their more boisterous enthusiasms. Bernabéu apologised for (but did not explain) the 11-1 match and, briefly, all was harmonious.

This cordiality lasted until the final Liga game of the 1943/44 season at Les Corts. With the referee reacting over-favourably towards the muscular spoiling tactics of Real, thereby generating accusations of back-handers, Real won 3-1. The pretence of friendship between the clubs was emphatically ended when Barcelona winger Riba had his arm broken after being kicked on the ground by a Real defender, the ref ignoring this wilful act of savagery. The artificial camaraderie between Real and Barcelona speedily evaporated, and hostility was back on the agenda.

Bankruptcy looms

Real Madrid claimed two more top-three places in the 1940s (1944/45 and 1948/49), but the aforementioned clubs still ruled the roost and Real declined – until the early 1950s – into a mid-table team. In 1947/48, they experienced the worst season of their history, when they narrowly avoided a relegation play-off and finished in 11th place, with only 21 points all season and scoring 41 while conceding 56 goals. After this shock, things began gradually to pick up.

Meanwhile, the astute Santiago Bernabéu had been busy making plans. It was not in his nature to be second-best, and Atlético Madrid – Athletic's new name, having split from the air force – were undoubtedly the better club (for the moment, anyway) in Madrid. Also, at the end of the disastrous 1943/44 season, and having been defeated in the Copa final by Athletic Bilbao, Real Madrid were virtually bankrupt.

Bernabéu was a proud and complex man: an ex-player, centralist and pro-Nationalist who had fallen out on several occasions with Franco. He was an authoritarian figure but also someone capable of deep empathy with his players. He was a sharp, quick-witted businessman who also had contacts at a high level in Madrid's banking, commercial and legal worlds. He was friendly with many of the club's influential socios. And he began to cultivate these contacts.

The Nuevo Chamartin Stadium

Bernabéu then unveiled his plans for the construction of a major new stadium for Real Madrid, located close to the Chamartin.

The idea was widely regarded as nonsensical and wholly inappropriate for a 'little club' such as Real, whose home attendance rarely rose above 16,000. However, receiving favourable credit terms, he acquired a plot of land of around 5 hectares on the Avenida del Generalissimo Franco to the north of the city, calculating that this was the direction in which Madrid's commercial life was heading. His reasoning proved correct, as today the thoroughfare is Avenida Castellana and is the main financial area and most prestigious address in the city.

Work began on the site in October 1944, and the Nuevo Chamartin was inaugurated in December 1947 with a game against Portugal's Os Belenenses. Two weeks later, Real's first Liga game in the new stadium was a 5-1 defeat of Athletic Bilbao watched by over 75,000 spectators, the biggest-ever crowd in Spain until then. Three months after the completion of the New Chamartin, Real had 8,000 socios. One year later, and despite the club's desperate flirtation with relegation, the number of members had risen to 43,000.

Bernabéu, however, was not neglecting the team. In 1947/48, with the assistance of his confidant the club's PR man Raimundo Saporto, Real bought in such quality players as midfielders

Miguel Muñoz from Celta de Vigo and Luis Molowny from Las Palmas. Both played for the club for ten years before embarking on distinguished coaching careers with Real, other clubs and their country. Saporto also attempted to acquire Ladislao Kubala, but Barcelona were quicker off the mark in signing the Hungarian genius.

Alfredo joins Real

To amend slightly a line from the poet T.S. Eliot in one of his early works, *The Love Song of J. Alfred Prufrock*:

In the room the players come and go
Talking of Di Stéfano.

Between 1947/48 and 1952/53, Barcelona (four titles) and Atlético Madrid (two titles) between them claimed the leadership of La Liga. Real were catching up with both, but six consecutive years of acting as the underdog to two of their long-term rivals was becoming hard for Madridismo pride to bear.

However, although Real's 50th anniversary coincided with Barcelona's dominant status in Primera, at the club's celebrations Bernabéu discovered a player who would profoundly change Real's future and ensure that not only players were 'talking of Di Stéfano'.

Bernabéu had invited the pre-eminent Latin American club Millonarios of Bogota to add lustre to the anniversary. The Colombian side's star was undoubtedly Alfredo Di Stéfano, a 23-year-old Argentinian. He had had disagreements with his Argentine club River Plate before travelling north to join the wealthy, if unofficial, Millonarios. A powerful, skilful player, he was a midfield dynamo, ruthless goalscorer and determined defender: one of the first 'total footballers'. After a long conversation with Di Stéfano on the evening before the game, Bernabéu observed to a colleague that 'this man smells of good football'. The game revealed to Bernabéu that Di Stéfano was indeed a special player and that this commanding Argentine was the man to turn around the fortunes of his ailing Real.

Di Stéfano has been eulogised at such length and by so many knowledgeable commentators that, particularly in a book of this nature, it is impossible to write anything about the man which has not previously been expressed innumerable times. So, I'll restrict myself to saying that he was one of the greatest footballers of all time and, without his masterly presence on the pitch over the coming few years, it is unlikely that Real would have become the most powerful and successful club in European football.

Again, there exist almost as many words on the frequently devious and protracted disagreements and disputes between Barcelona and Real over the ownership of Di Stéfano as there are articles to be found on the man himself. So, I will take the (self-indulgent) opportunity of repeating what I wrote in my book *Life in La Liga*: 'suffice to say that, at the critical moment, Barcelona blinked, while Real maintained its gaze'.

Gale warning

Alfredo Di Stéfano signed for Real in September 1953 and in his first month scored four goals in Real's 5-0 Liga win at the Nuevo Chamartin. The opponents? Who else but Barcelona? As a result of what was to follow the Argentinian's arrival at Real, football in Spain and Europe would be fundamentally and irrevocably changed, as would the Continent's sociopolitical and cultural attitudes towards the Spanish nation.

At the conclusion of season 1953/54, Real won La Liga for the first time in 20 years and ended four points ahead of Barcelona. In 1950, La Liga had expanded to 16 clubs, and the top scorer in his first season was Di Stéfano – now known by fans as 'The Blond Arrow' – with 29 goals.

Shortly before the arrival of Di Stéfano, Bernabéu had snapped up from Rácing de Santander an explosively fast, young left-winger, Francisco ('Paco') Gento. The young Cantabrian had a relatively quiet opening season, but the arrival in 1953/54 of new manager José Villalonga, and his discussions with Di Stéfano and Bernabéu, soon changed this. Di Stéfano suggested that the acquisition of his fellow Argentinian Hector Rial, an inside-left and elegant passer and header of the ball, would complement both his and Gento's left-sided threat.

In season 1954/55, this is precisely what happened. Gento, known by fans as 'la Galerna' (the Gale), sped down the left wing, supplied by Rial's immaculate talents on the ball, and sent over pinpoint crosses for Di Stéfano and Molowny to convert. On occasion, he would also cut inside the increasingly breathless defenders and shoot with either foot. With their strong defence and incomparable attack, Real again won Primera that season, with Di Stéfano scoring 25 Liga goals and Real finishing five points ahead of Barcelona.

Also, that season the members voted to rename the ground after Santiago Bernabéu, in honour of his 43-year committed service to the club. Finally, everything was falling into place for Real and for Bernabéu, but even this battle-hardened optimist was unprepared for what was to follow over the coming five years.

A tournament for champions

In December 1954, English League champions Wolves recovered from 0-2 down against Hungarian side Honved to win 3-2. Although the game was a friendly and played at Molineux, the English team were hailed by the *Daily Mail* as 'Champions of the World'. This triumphalist gauntlet was eagerly picked up by Gabriel Hanot, editor of French sports paper *L'Équipe*, who had long been a proponent of a European cup competition.

At an April 1955 meeting in Paris, which was attended by an enthusiastic Bernabéu, Hanot laid out to a number of European clubs his plan for an annual competition between the top Continental clubs; a tournament which would decide who really were the 'champions' of Europe. The following month, FIFA ratified the proposal and passed the organisation of the project to UEFA. So was born the European Champion Clubs' Cup – the European Cup – which would consist of each participating country's national champions drawn against each other on a knockout, home-and-away basis.

The first season of the European Cup, comprising clubs from 16 countries, kicked off in September 1955. In that first season, not all the teams had won their national league, some teams declined, and a few national bodies were sceptical. England, for instance, did not send a team on the stated grounds that the new competition would interfere with their domestic schedule.

UEFA had to convince these teams and countries of the value and status of the competition. This they very quickly did.

European Cup, 1955/56: La Prima

Real's first game in the European Cup was on 8 September 1955 in Geneva. Their opponents were Servette, a Swiss side managed by Karl Rappan who invented 'the bolt' defence, forerunner of the stultifying 'catenaccio' system. Two second-half goals without reply – Muñoz scoring Real's first-ever goal in European competition – were followed by a 5-0 Real win at the Bernabéu, Di Stéfano opening his European account with two goals. So far, so good.

The quarter-final was trickier. Real were drawn against communist Yugoslavia's Partizan Belgrade, and Franco was not happy with the pairing. Saporta had to use all his persuasive guile on the dictator, but he managed it. The game went ahead on Christmas Day afternoon (the floodlights were pending) in a packed, festive Bernabéu, and the celebrations continued long after Real's 4-0 defeat of Partizan. The fourth goal proved to be a wise move by Di Stéfano as, in the end-January return game in sub-zero temperatures and on a frozen pitch in Belgrade, Real were fortunate to lose only 3-0 and squeeze through to the semi-final.

In mid-April, Real faced another daunting test, this time against a resurgent AC Milan, with the Italian club's forwards – Uruguay's Juan Schiaffino and Sweden's Nils Liedholm – posing particular threats. In the Bernabéu, another 130,000 fans watched as both these players scored to equalise at half-time, but Real emerged as 4-2 winners. Two weeks later at the San Siro, a cautious, more defensive Real gave away two late penalties, but their solitary goal was enough for an aggregate 5-4 victory.

On 13 June 1956 at the Parc des Princes, Real faced France's leading side Stade de Reims, whose attack was spearheaded by the brilliant Raymond Kopa, in the first-ever European Cup final. Two goals down after only 12 minutes, Real came back through Di Stéfano and Rial. Reims went ahead in the second half, but Marquitos equalised, a rare goal from the big Real defender. With ten minutes remaining, Gento laid on a second goal for Rial. The game ended 4-3 to Real, and the Spanish club had won the inaugural European Cup (La Prima).

The tournament had been an outstanding team performance from Real but, as *France Soir* observed, 'the main reason for Madrid's victory was Di Stéfano'. However, Villalonga and Di Stéfano were concerned that the thrust of their attack emanated from the left wing, and they needed a balance from the right. So, Raymond Kopa, who had impressed in the final, joined Real over the 1956 close season. 'After what I've seen in this game', said Kopa, 'I don't know why they want me,' but he soon settled into his new role.

European Cup, 1956/57: La Segunda

Real· had won the European trophy, but, exhausted by their efforts, they ended the 1955/56 season third in La Liga behind Athletic Bilbao and Barcelona, albeit with Di Stéfano again top domestic scorer.

In its first season, the European Cup had been a great success, with over 1 million spectators and a total of 127 goals scored. Six more countries (including England) entered their national champions for the 1956/57 competition. As title holders, Real were again in the Cup and given a preliminary-round bye. Their first tie was against Rapid Vienna.

At the Bernabéu, they achieved a 4-2 win, but at Rapid's Prater Stadium they found themselves 3-0 down at half-time, courtesy of an Ernst Happel hat-trick. Di Stéfano scored in the second half to make the game 5-5 on aggregate. As extra time was permitted only in the final, a financial inducement to Rapid to locate the play-off at the Bernabéu was accepted by the Austrians, and Real won 2-0.

Having disposed of Nice 6-2 in the quarter-final, they then found themselves in mid-April 1957 facing Manchester United – the 'Busby Babes' – who were the first English side in the competition, having won the English League by 11 points. With mounted police and running fights around the Bernabéu, and another capacity crowd in the stadium, Real ended 3-1 victors. In Manchester, and despite Busby's pre-match claim that 'we'll knock them out', the Babes were 2-0 behind at half-time, thanks to Real's tactical and individual superiority and strikes by Kopa and Rial. Although United scored twice in the second half, Real won 5-3 on aggregate and were again in the final.

On 30 May 1957, Real met Italian champions Fiorentina in the final at the Bernabéu. An essentially defensive side, Fiorentina held out against the Madrid ball artists until the 67th minute, when Mateos was fouled and Di Stéfano converted the penalty. Six minutes later, Gento chipped over the Italian keeper, and a dour game ended 2-0 to Real who claimed their second, successive European Cup (La Segunda). Generalissimo Franco presented captain Muñoz, who retired from playing after the game, with the trophy.

Watching the game was Uruguayan José Santamaria, Real's annual 'name' recruit. A tall, commanding centre-half nicknamed 'The Wall', he strengthened the defence and was a technically gifted supplier to the marauding forward line, particularly Di Stéfano. Domestically, Real also won La Liga, five points in front of Sevilla, although they lost 6-1 to Barcelona in the Copa, a tournament which appeared to be something of an irritating distraction for this magnificent team.

Real Madrid line up before the 1957 European Cup final against Fiorentina at the Bernabéu.

European Cup, 1957/58: La Tercera

As the third season of the European Cup began, more countries had entered the tournament, the number of spectators had doubled, and Gabriel Hanot's vision had been vindicated. Under new manager Luis Carniglia, Real continued to demonstrate why they were the undisputed European champions.

First, they brushed aside Royal Antwerp – Rial scoring a hat-trick at home – with an emphatic 8-1 win. Then, in the quarter-final, they were drawn against Liga runners-up Sevilla. At the Bernabéu in January, Real humiliated the clearly inferior Andalucian side by rattling in eight goals with no reply, Di Stéfano becoming the first player in the Cup to score four in a game. A 2-2 result in Seville meant an aggregate 10-2 win for Real and a 50-year wait for Sevilla to summon up the courage again to enter the Cup. The semi-final ended in a 4-2 defeat of Hungary's Vasas, Di Stéfano securing another hat-trick.

It was a different matter, however, in the Heysel Stadium on 28 May 1958 when Real met Italian champions AC Milan in the final. Both sides had scored 26 goals to reach this stage, and Milan were a respected and worthy opponent for Real, as the Spanish side had discovered two years previously. The game was a tense, edgy encounter of attack and counter-attack which, after 90 minutes, was deadlocked at 2-2, Rial and Di Stéfano having scored for the holders. Both teams went close in extra time, and the stalemate was broken in the 107th minute when a Gento shot rebounded to the Real winger who then made sure with his next attempt. The game ended 3-2 to Real, ensuring a third successive European trophy (La Tercera) for the Spanish club. This was the most challenging game to date for Real in the European Cup. Di Stéfano later commented, 'we stole it from Milan . . . it was hard going'.

This was Real's second doblete in succession, having again won La Liga, this time beating second-placed city rival Atlético Madrid by three points. The two Madrid clubs would meet in the forthcoming 1958/59 European Cup, and Real would have in their team this year's new signing Ferenc Puskás.

Di Stéfano celebrates as the winning goal hits the net in the final.

The 'Galloping Major'

An overweight 31-year-old, Puskás was nonetheless one of the very few European footballers whose influence and ability at Real could equal that of Di Stéfano. A former inside-left with the Hungarian army team Honved – from which derived his nickname – he was also a dominant figure in the Hungarian national side which destroyed England 6-3 and 7-1 in 1953 and 1954. Playing abroad when the Soviet tanks rolled into Budapest in 1956, Puskás then remained in voluntary exile and, as a result, was banned by UEFA from playing.

At Bernabéu's request, Saporta 'persuaded' UEFA to rescind the ban, and in August 1958 Puskás joined Real even though the board had voted against signing him. Assuming the inside-left position of an unhappy Rial, who then played a secondary role until his departure in 1961, Puskás shrugged off his recent inactivity and became a perfect complement to Di Stéfano, allowing the Argentinian to adopt a more permanent attacking role while Puskás provided the guile and intelligence in linking up with and supplying him. Puskás also possessed a ferocious left-foot shot and was known by Real fans as 'Cañoncito Pum!' ('Little Cannon Bang!'). In January 1959, they both scored hat-tricks in the 10-1 hammering of Las Palmas, and he and Di Stéfano, alongside Kopa and Gento, devastated defences across Europe during the late 1950s.

In his first season, Puskás scored 21 Liga goals, second only to Di Stéfano's Liga tally of 23, although Barcelona won Primera that year. In total, Puskás scored 240 goals in his 260 appearances for Real: not bad going for a tubby, ageing inside-left.

European Cup, 1958/59: La Cuarta

Real were, as champions, back in the fourth European Cup. Having overcome Turkish champions Besiktas, they faced Wiener Sport-Club, who had provided the tournament's shock result by eliminating Agnelli's Juventus 7-0 in Vienna. A 0-0 draw saw Puskás sent off for retaliation.

As Di Stéfano had already received his marching orders in the home win over Besiktas, it seemed that the close marking and fouling, which was now often employed against star players in the European game, was generating frustrated reactions from the recipients. Real's 7-1 win at the Bernabéu, with Di Stéfano scoring four goals, was designed to teach the impudent Austrians how the game should be played.

Atlético Madrid, for so long the second-best club in the Spanish capital, put up a strong fight in the Bernabéu semi-final but lost 2-1. Up the road at the Metropolitano, the 'mattress makers' had the temerity to defeat their more illustrious neighbours 1-0 and force a replay. At Zaragoza, however, normality was restored, and Di Stéfano and Puskás ensured a 2-1 win. Atlético were to regain a degree of status in Madrid when they defeated Real in both the 1960 and 1961 Copa finals.

In the deciding game at Stuttgart's Neckarstadion on 3 June 1959, with 72,000 in attendance, Stade de Reims were once more the opposition. The French team had a forward line containing Just Fontaine, lead scorer at the 1958 World Cup finals, but they adopted an unpleasantly over-physical strategy, and it was probably just as well that Puskás was absent due to injury. The game was an uninspiring spectacle, but Mateos and, of course, Di Stéfano scored in the 2-0 win. It was Kopa's last game for the club and the last time a French side would be in the final until St Étienne appeared in 1976. It was now Real's fourth European Cup in succession (La Cuarta).

Real Madrid captain Zarraga holds aloft the European Cup in 1959.

European Cup, 1959/60: La Quinta

Despite all that Real have achieved since then, 1960 is remembered as the club's greatest year. In particular, it is fondly recalled for that year's European Cup final, which has been hailed as the finest combination of unparalleled skill, team empathy and individual brilliance that has ever been displayed on a football pitch.

Over the summer of 1959, Real had brought in two Brazilians: Canário, a ball-playing right-winger who replaced Kopa; and Didi, an attacking midfielder who didn't stay long at the club. The third 'name' import was 25-year-old inside-right Luis Del Sol from Real Betis.

On their way to the final, Real Madrid began by defeating Luxembourg's Jeunesse Esch 12-2 and then Nice 6-3. Unusually, they lost 2-3 to the French champions in the first game, but a 4-0 win at the Bernabéu saw them comfortably through to the semi-final, where their rivals Barcelona awaited.

Liga winners the previous season, the Catalan club had already inflicted a 7-1 defeat on AC Milan in the first round and an even more humiliating 9-2 routing of English champions Wolves in the quarter-finals. Under the eccentric but effective management of Helenio Herrera, Barcelona considered themselves the leading Spanish team and were irritated by Real's hogging of the headlines.

The two clubs met in April 1960, and Herrera's decision to drop Kubala and Czibor for the first leg over a bonus dispute did not help the Catalan cause, nor did it endear him to the crowd or the board. Real eliminated Barcelona 6-2 on aggregate, with two 3-1 defeats and two goals apiece from Di Stéfano and Puskás, and they marched on to their fifth successive European Cup final (La Quinta).

The second leg at Camp Nou was Barcelona's first home defeat for two years, and it was described in the press as 'Herrera's Waterloo'. The manager was fired and he joined Inter Milan who, following Herrera's ultra-defensive tactics, would meet Real in four years' time in the European Cup final. That was to be Di Stéfano's last ever appearance for Real Madrid.

'Vikings' enthral Hampden

'Real Madrid strolls through Europe as the Vikings once did, destroying everything in its path.'

This quote from *The Times* after the 1960 European Cup final at Glasgow's Hampden Park was clearly written by an awestruck observer of the game in search of an historic parallel for the football match he had just witnessed.

The *Daily Mail* observed that 'the thousands of people at the ground must have thought they were dreaming' when watching Real's astonishing play. Similar hyperbolic sentiments were echoed across Europe, with *France Soir* hailing the Real performance as 'magisterial ballet' after the Spanish team's breathtaking artistry on the football pitch destroyed West German champions Eintracht Frankfurt 7-3.

Scotland's old national stadium had crammed in a massive crowd of 127,000, and millions more were watching on TV, as the game kicked off on that Wednesday evening of 18 May 1960. Many in the ground supported Real, as local club Rangers had been crushed 12-4 by Eintracht in the semi-finals and 'Gers supporters were seeking revenge. But such was the scintillating performance of the Spanish side that their anger towards the Germans perhaps turned to pity, or at least relief that Rangers were not at the receiving end.

Although the Germans opened the scoring and then hit the bar, they were 3-1 down by half-time. In the second period,

Puskás claimed three more within 20 minutes and Di Stéfano almost immediately added the seventh. Eintracht played well enough to have defeated most club sides, and they picked up two consolation goals, but they were outclassed by Real's superiority. Puskás scored four while Di Stéfano had to content himself with a hat-trick. At the end of the game, Real went on an impromptu lap of honour round Hampden, and the huge crowd rose to salute the champions.

Puskas scores Real's fourth goal from the penalty spot during the 1960 European Cup final. *PA*

Hampden, 1960: the aftermath

To this day, no European Cup or Champions League final has produced an outcome of ten goals, nor has any other European club won the trophy in five successive years. These Real players had done more to boost the image of Spanish football and, by association, Franco's Spain than virtually anything previously promoted by the dictator and his government.

Also, Real's masterclass had demonstrated the relative inadequacy of the British game, and had finally shattered the cosy, self-deluding British clubs' belief in their own innate superiority in European football. By so doing, and judging by the generally improved British performances in European Cups afterwards, it can reasonably be argued that Real in 1960 at Hampden did a service to club football in Britain.

That final was a magnificent swansong for the Real team, as other European sides – particularly Benfica, AC Milan and Inter Milan – were lying in wait. Ex-captain and now manager Miguel Muñoz was to remain in his post for the following 14 years, but several of the players were ageing. A younger generation would soon be ready to don Real's all-white strip.

The Real team in the unforgettable 1960 final was: Dominguez, Marquitos, Pachin, Vidal, Santamaria, Zarraga, Canário, Del Sol, Di Stéfano, Puskás and Gento.

Real Madrid celebrate with the European Cup after beating
Eintracht Frankfurt 7-3 in the 1960 final at Hampden Park. *PA*

A brief historical interjection

After the Second World War, Europe and the major Western powers had refused to recognise Franco's Spain, but this began to change in 1953 when the USA dropped its isolation policy toward the country. The USA had remained 'neutral' during the Spanish Civil War, although it turned a blind eye to one of its citizens who supplied fuel to Franco and thereby established his company, Texaco, as a leading multinational corporation.

Spain's location at the junction of the Mediterranean and the Atlantic, combined with its virulent anti-communist stance, made it a potential ally against the Soviet Union, so the US and Spanish governments signed the Pact of Madrid, in which US air bases were to be established across the country. The USA then formally recognised the Spanish dictatorship through the resumption of diplomatic relations. This was a triumph for Franco.

It also led to Spain's acceptance back into the Western fold, with the country joining the United Nations in 1955 and, by 1959, the International Monetary Fund (IMF) and the Organisation for Economic Cooperation and Development. The IMF connection was instrumental in Spain ditching its policy of autarky (economic self-sufficiency) in favour of economic and, to a degree, social liberalisation.

In 1959, the recently created Ministry of Tourism abolished entry visas for tourists and devalued the peseta, making Spain's many beaches easier to reach and affordable. The initial result was that the number of tourists soared from 4 million in 1960 to 18 million in 1967. This ruined many coastal villages, Benidorm being an obvious example, but the isolationism began to fade, to the benefit of tourists and locals alike.

What has all this to do with Real? The club had long been regarded as the 'Regime Team', benefiting from Bernabéu's connections with the government and acting as unofficial ambassadors and supporters for Francoism. However, there is little basis for these attacks other than a deep distrust of centralism in certain quarters. Many will argue that, although there may be an 'elective affinity' between Real's success and the requirements of the dictatorship, the actions of the latter did not further the cause of the former. In other words, Real could arguably have achieved their 'five-in-a-row' without any Francoist intervention.

Bernabéu had been a Nationalist, but he was his own man; and while Real may well have been favoured in certain respects, the football pitch shows little political allegiance. Indeed, a good number of Real's players would have been incensed at such pro-Francoist allegations.

Although it is difficult to discover the truth behind the critiques, Real do appear to have been victims of envy for their achievements as much as for their suggested links with Francoism.

'Famous Five': the declining years

In the words of the Prophet in the Old Testament Book of *Ecclesiastes*: 'To every thing there is a season, and a time to every purpose under the heaven.' Real's European domination had to end at some point. But its conclusion was rather abrupt, and its instigators were not exactly whom the champions had in mind.

Fresh from their Hampden triumph, they were drawn against Liga winners Barcelona in Round 1 of the 1960/61 European Cup. With a forward line of Kubala, Kocsis, Evaristo, Suárez and Czibor, the Catalans were formidable, particularly as the injured Santamaria was unavailable to keep an eye on Real's defence.

The first leg was at the Bernabéu on 9 November. Mateos and Gento had scored to put Real 2-1 ahead, but in the final minutes Kocsis fell in the box. Referee Arthur Ellis awarded a penalty, despite heated protestations from Real's defenders, and Suárez scored the equaliser. This was the first European Cup game that Real had not won at home since the inception of the tournament.

A couple of weeks later in Barcelona's recently constructed Camp Nou, another English ref, Reg Leafe, oversaw the second leg, disallowing four of five Real goals while permitting both of Barcelona's. A Canário strike at the end of the match was all Real were allowed in their 2-1 defeat. Beaten 4-3 on aggregate, Real were out of the European Cup at the earliest stage.

Bernabéu commented that referee Leafe had been Barcelona's best player. The referee had indeed made dubious judgements during the game, and his face apparently formed the centrepiece of Madrid dartboards for many years. The boot was now on the other foot.

The chant of *Asi, asi, asi, gana el Madrid* (That's the way Madrid win) was apparently first heard from Sporting Gijón fans. Thereafter, it was sung by fans of other opposing teams who alleged the city boys from the capital used their wealthy contacts to 'influence' matches, that they were favoured by referees, were very bad losers and were often simply lucky. Despite the questionable refereeing decisions in Barca's favour in both games, similar mocking chants were absent from the Catalan celebrations.

Domestic dominance: the 1960s

A consolation for Real was that in the 1960s they virtually took over La Liga. During this decade, Real won La Liga five times in succession, came second behind an intrusive Atlético Madrid in 1965/66, won the following three titles, and were again forced into second place by a determined Atlético in 1969/70.

Other clubs – mainly Barcelona but also Athletic Bilbao, Real Zaragoza, Real Betis, Real Oviedo, Español, Las Palmas and Sevilla – made the top three over these ten years, but Real were implacable and virtually immoveable in their dominance of La Liga.

However, in this decade they won only one Copa: in 1962 against Sevilla. Moreover, their domination of the European Cup was reaching its end, at least for the time being. Di Stéfano, Puskás, Santamaria and the other members of the 'Famous Five' were now significantly older, and even Gento was slowing down. But in 1961/62, the season following the defeat by Barcelona, this legendary and determined team reached another final.

They brushed aside Vasas and Odense, the latter by 12-0. Real then needed a replay against Juventus to achieve a 6-0 result over Standard Liège, and they were back in the final. Benfica, conquerors of Barcelona the previous year, were their opponents in Amsterdam on 2 May. In a fast, exciting game, described as 'the night of the long shots', by the 38th minute Puskás had a hat-trick, becoming the only player to have achieved this in two European Cup finals. With the score 3-3 as the second half began, the younger Benfica side were increasingly dominating the match. Within four minutes, 19-year-old recent signing Eusebio scored two for Benfica, and these goals wrapped it up. Benfica lifted the European Cup, and Real Madrid had lost their first final.

The following year, Real lost in Round 1 to Anderlecht by a 4-3 margin, so new faces were required. Del Sol moved to Juventus, and in came forward Amario 'the Wizard' Amancio from Deportivo de La Coruña and defender Zoco from Osasuna, among others. Puskás, Di Stéfano and Gento remained the attacking mainstays. However, the two newcomers were also to become legendary figures at the club.

Anyone seen Alfredo?

To recover from the unseemly dismissal by Anderlecht and to prepare for the coming Liga season, Real travelled in August 1963 to Venezuela for a friendly tournament.

Shortly after arriving in Caracas, Di Stéfano was staying at the Hotel Potomac when he received a 6 am phone call from the hotel lobby. His roommate Santamaria grunted and went back to sleep, but the Argentinian answered and was told to come downstairs to be interviewed by two policemen, so he did. He left the hotel at gunpoint with the 'policemen' and was driven to a nearby flat, where he met Paul del Rio, the leader of the Armed Forces of National Liberation (FALN), who told Di Stéfano that he'd been kidnapped. The group needed publicity in their struggle with President Romulo Betancourt's government, and what could generate more such press coverage than snatching Europe's best-known footballer?

Although at first the kidnapee 'thought they were going to kill me', he was assured that he would soon be freed, and they all settled down to play cards and dominoes. Meanwhile, the kidnap had made front-page headlines across European newspapers, and such was the furore that Betancourt ordered tanks onto the streets. Di Stéfano was set free two days later, went straight to the Spanish Embassy and was reunited with his club, for whom he played the next day.

Almost 40 years later, Di Stéfano was invited by his kidnapper for a friendly chat. He declined, although he forgave them, telling *El Pais* that 'they were trying to improve things'.

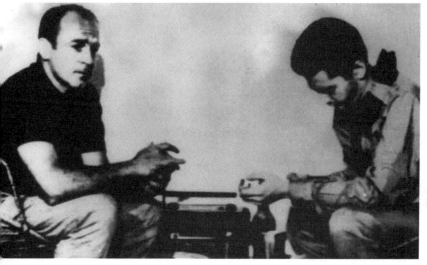

Alfredo Di Stéfano sits next to Paul del Rio, his kidnapper in 1963. *EFE*

Real v Catenaccio

A growing number of European teams had begun to adopt a style of football which was the antithesis of Real's attacking model of rampaging forwards with supply from an effective, attacking defence and a creatively obliging midfield.

Increasingly, the emphasis was on defensive play and swift counter-attacking, in attempts to emulate the growing success of some Italian clubs. Inter Milan, under Herrera, were the prime exponents of what became known as *catenaccio* (the bolt). This was a defensive extension of Herbert Chapman's 'WM' formation when he managed Arsenal, and it was further developed by Austrian coach Karl Rappan.

Catenaccio consisted of a *libero* (sweeper) patrolling behind four man-marking defenders, a three- or four-man midfield, and one or perhaps two forwards. The idea was to absorb opposing attacks, ensure that no goals were conceded, score on swift counter-attacks, and then protect the lead. It was boring to watch but, with the right players, it seemed to work.

In 1967, Celtic joyfully destroyed catenaccio in their demolition of the Inter defence in the European Cup final. A few Inter players were in tears towards the end of the game, as they were totally unprepared for the constant interchanging of position, imagination and speed of Celtic's attack. Some years later, Bayern Munich's Franz Beckenbauer repositioned the libero as an attacker, and the system adapted accordingly.

Herrera seeks revenge

Earlier in the 1960s, catenaccio had certainly worked for Inter Milan, as was demonstrated in their 1964 European Cup final against Real.

Real had once more arrived at the final, this time by dismissing Rangers 7-0 and Dinamo Bucharest 8-4. They then squeezed through 4-3 against a tough AC Milan and took apart FC Zurich 8-1 in the semi-final. However, they had either taken their eyes off European footballing developments or been distracted by their failed attempts to land Pelé, as they were defeated by a vengeful Herrera and his defensive Inter Milan.

The manager had deployed his full range of catenaccio tactics at Vienna's Prater Stadium against Real in the final on 27 May 1964. Inter Milan's tight, well-disciplined defence and their roaming sweeper stymied the Real attack – a forward line containing such goalscoring supremos as Amancio, Puskás and Di Stéfano – with the result that Real could manage only one goal, through Felo. However, Mazzola on the counter-attack – a hallmark of catenaccio – scored two for the Italians, Milani scored another, and Inter won 3-1 to claim the European Cup.

Real had again failed to get their hands on what, only a few short years ago, they had regarded as 'their' trophy.

Exit of the old guard

In summer 1964, Muñoz and Bernabéu had to come to terms with Di Stéfano's age and diminishing ability. He was now 38 years old and appreciably slower than when he'd arrived at Real 11 years earlier. He had to go. He was offered a major role on the technical staff, said Real, but turned it down. Not true, said Di Stéfano, who wanted a new playing contract.

In June 1964, after an emotionally bitter falling-out with Bernabéu, who insisted that Di Stéfano would not enter the Bernabéu Stadium while he (as president) still lived, the Argentinian left Real on a free transfer and with bad grace on both sides. He had won 11 Liga titles and five European Cups for Real and had in every sense revolutionised the club. He joined Español and then moved into management. After coaching several clubs, he arrived back as manager of Real and helped to initiate the next 'golden generation' – 'La Quinta del Buitre' – in the early 1980s.

The following year in the second round of the Cup, Real could only draw 2-2 away with Kilmarnock – the Scottish club's only venture into the tournament – but won 5-1 in Madrid. However, by now veterans, Puskás and Santamaria, who both played against Killie, never again played for Real. It was time for younger, different players to take over from the club legends. As they showed in their 1965/66 European Cup journey, they were more than capable replacements for the old boys.

The 'Ye-Ye' years

By the mid-1960s, Real were entering the post-Di Stéfano era, and Spain was changing. The exponential growth in tourism, the expanding economy and the country's reintegration into Europe were accompanied by a growing social liberalism, cautious though this may have been. The grim austerity of the post-Civil War years was being replaced by a sense of positivity and optimism, as the country – particularly its younger, more defiant members – was increasingly influenced by the socio-cultural movements affecting the rest of the Western world.

As an indication of such change, the Beatles played Madrid in July 1965. Their music, particularly 'She Loves You' with its 'yeah, yeah, yeah' refrain, was played on radio stations across Spain, and it seemed to mirror the new mood within the country. Real, too, had been acquiring younger players with fresher, more flexible attitudes than their illustrious predecessors'. Several of these players, complete with Beatles wigs, appeared in an early-1966 photo which was printed on the cover of national magazines.

The new Real players were immediately christened the 'Ye-Ye' team, a nickname which well captured the nature of their confident and stylish approach to the game.

European Cup, 1965/66: La Sexta

Two players who became integral parts of the 'Ye-Ye' side were Amancio and Zoco, both of whom had played in the European Cup final against Inter Milan two years previously. Since then, Real had brought together several other new players.

These included José Martinez Sánchez (known as 'Pirri'), a multi-talented midfielder/sweeper acquired from Granada. From the Real youth system came three locals: Rámon Moreno Grasso, a forward with the unenviable task of taking over Di Stéfano's position; Manuel Velázquez, a quick-thinking midfielder with the equally thankless role of following in Puskás's footsteps; and Pedro De Felipe, who was to be the next Santamaria. The only permanent team member from the earlier regime was Gento, now, at the age of 32 years, perhaps less of a 'Gale' but still capable of creating a storm of confusion in opposing defences.

Real had won their fifth successive Liga the previous season and were back in the European Cup. They had eliminated Feyenoord and, as mentioned, Kilmarnock, and two goals apiece from Amancio and Gento saw off a troublesome Anderlecht in the quarter-final. In the semi-final, they again met Inter Milan, who were aiming for their third title in succession, and a Pirri goal squeezed them through at the Bernabéu. Although Herrera threatened that 'Madrid will burn in the San Siro', another Pirri goal got Real to the final in a dourly defensive match.

At the Heysel Stadium on 11 May 1966 the opposition was Partizan Belgrade, a club whom Real Madrid had last encountered and narrowly defeated in a 1955/56 European Cup quarter-final. Real began nervously but grew in confidence, even when Partizan opened the scoring. Real then launched a no-holds-barred attack and scored twice in the last 20 minutes to win the game and the European Cup. Real had again scaled the heights of European club football to claim their sixth trophy (La Sexta) and they had achieved this, for the first time, with 11 players who were all Spanish.

This record-breaking performance, however, was to be the club's last appearance in the final for 15 years, and it would be their last European Cup trophy for 32 long years.

Francisco Gento lifts the European Cup in 1966. *PA*

The end of the affair . . . for now

The years immediately following La Sexta are known by Real Madrid as 'La época del desierto' (the wilderness years). For most other European clubs, a glittering ten-year record such as Real's would instead be named 'time for a well-deserved rest', but Real had grown so used to winning at the highest level that 'wilderness' it became.

In Round 2 of the 1966/67 European Cup, Real defeated 1860 Munich 3-2, but in the quarter-final they were eliminated 3-0 by Inter Milan. However, having won La Liga in 1966/67 and suffering only two losses – to Barcelona and Zaragoza – they again realised the increasing strength of the opposition in the following season's European Cup.

In Round 1, Real travelled to Amsterdam to face the respected Rinus Michels's Ajax and his star pupil, 21-year-old Johan Cruyff, the latter being a name Real would have good reason to remember over the coming years. Cruyff and Pirri both scored in the 1-1 draw. At the Bernabéu, the seemingly ageless Gento struck first, Ajax equalised, and Veloso – a striker bought from Deportivo de La Coruña a couple of years previously – dribbled his way through the entire Dutch defence to smash home Real's winner from 25 yards.

In the following rounds, Real disposed of Hvidvore and Sparta Prague, Amancio scoring a ten-minute hat-trick against the Czech side to reach the semi-final. Waiting for them were the English champions Manchester United.

The Busby Babes return

Ten years after the Munich disaster, Matt Busby had rebuilt United into one of Europe's finest teams. The heart of the side was Charlton, Best, Stiles and Law (who was injured for much of the season), as well as Foulkes, Sadler and Herd. They were a formidable proposition, and the two games were a 'clash of the giants' of European football.

The first leg in April 1968 at Old Trafford was a sell-out, with an estimated 150 million watching on TV. With Amancio suspended, Real showed their defensive edge. A Best goal kept the result to 1-0, which did not appear a sufficient lead for the frenzied cauldron of the Bernabéu.

Real were a different team at home. By half-time, Gento, Pirri and Amancio had scored, although Zoco conceded an own goal, to make the game 3-1 to Real. In the second period, United responded to Busby's plea to attack – 'Go out there and enjoy yourselves' – by scoring through Sadler. The tie was now level on aggregate. Close to the end, big centre-half Bill Foulkes, ignoring the screams from his bench to get back into defence, ran up the pitch and side-footed a Best cross into the net. The final whistle blew, United were in the final, and Real were out.

The Cup Winners' Cup?

Over the following two seasons – 1967/68 and 1968/69 – Real resumed their domestic dominance. In the latter season, for instance, they topped La Liga by 11 points over the briefly resurgent Las Palmas, and they were undefeated in their first 27 league games. Europe, however, was a problem. In both seasons, they reached no further than the second round of the European Cup, where they were eliminated by Rapid Vienna and Standard Liège respectively.

In 1969/70, therefore, when Real could only finish in sixth place in Primera, they were finally out of the following season's European Cup: the first time this had happened since the tournament began 14 years previously. However, their 3-1 victory over Valencia in the Copa del Generalissimo meant that they were now eligible for the 1970/71 European Cup Winners' Cup.

The Cup Winners' Cup – a knockout, home-and-away competition with the final being a one-off played on a neutral ground – for European domestic cup champions was first held in 1960/61 and was formally recognised by UEFA in 1963. It was absorbed into the UEFA Cup in 1999. Spanish club winners were Barcelona, Atlético Madrid, Valencia and Zaragoza. The Cup Winners' Cup was regarded by Bernabéu as a somewhat inferior tournament for a club of Real's status, and he saw the competition as 'slumming it'. But it was the only tournament left for Real in 1970/71, so he signed up for it.

Real reached the 1971 final by defeating Hibs 5-0, Wacker Innsbruck 2-1, Cardiff City 2-1 and PSV Eindhoven 2-1. None of these were emphatic scorelines against prestigious opposition, but the final against Chelsea, in mid-May 1971 in Athens, promised to be a more interesting test. In front of a 45,000 crowd, Osgood and Zoco scored but, as it remained 1-1 after extra time, a replay was needed.

Two days later, the clubs met at the same venue. Osgood and Dempsey put Chelsea 2-0 ahead on the night, and new signing from Málaga Sébastien Fleitas pulled one back for Real, but it was too late. Chelsea had claimed their first European trophy, and Real had once again failed in Europe.

The Guruceta affair

Although Real Madrid reached the Cup Winners' final, there remains a strong possibility that they should not even have qualified for this tournament.

In the quarter-final of the previous year's Copa del Generalissimo, Real were drawn to face Barcelona. In the first leg at the Bernabéu, Real achieved a comfortable 2-0 win to take to the Camp Nou, and it was in Catalonia that the trouble began.

Barcelona's Carles (Charlie) Rexach scored the opening goal. It was now 2-1 on aggregate. Then Real's Velázquez, on an attacking run, was tackled outside the Catalans' penalty area, and his powerful forward momentum carried him into it, where he fell over. The referee Emilio Guruceta, then regarded as one of Spain's best refs, awarded a penalty to Real instead of the free kick which the offence warranted. Everything then flared up, with Barcelona protesting for fully eight minutes, Éladio being sent off for being especially vociferous (and applauding ironically as he left the pitch), and the Catalan side threatening to leave the pitch.

Amancio scored the penalty, and the crowd began to throw bottles at the ref, chant anti-Madrid songs and launch pitch invasions. Such was the mayhem that Guruceta blew the final whistle several minutes early, and he and his two linesman spent that night in police custody 'for their own protection'. Barcelona accused Real of bribing the ref, while Bernabéu commented, 'What are they complaining about? It was a penalty.' However, there was no hard or firm evidence available (although Velázquez later said that he was fouled outside the box), the result stood at 3-1, and Real went through, eventually to win the Copa. Guruceta was disqualified for six months for 'disturbance of public order'. He never again refereed a Barcelona game and he died in a car crash in 1987.

Ten years after the game, Anderlecht admitted bribing a ref before a match against Nottingham Forest, which Forest lost. The Belgian club was banned for one year from European football, and the 'bent referee' was Emilio Guruceta.

Think what you will.

Chaos on the pitch at the Camp Nou following Guruceta's controversial penalty award to Real. *Coleccionable LV Gran album del Barça*

Changes at the Bernabéu

After the 1971 Cup Winners' Cup final defeat by Chelsea, Gento hung up his boots and retired from the game. One of the greatest left-wingers in footballing history, he had spent 18 years with Real and won six European Cups and 12 Liga titles with the club. But age had finally caught up with the 39-year-old 'Gale'. Other players who left the club that summer included left-back Manuel Sanchís and keeper Antonio Betancort, both of whom had marked up ten fruitful years at the Bernabéu.

From Racing Santander arrived the 19-year-old forward Carlos Santillana, who was to be a regular goalscorer with the club for the following 17 seasons and played every game in season 1971/72. Real Madrid led La Liga, now enlarged to 18 clubs, for virtually the entirety of that season and they won back the league title, with a re-energised Valencia in second place. Valencia had claimed the title the previous season, while Real had managed only fourth place.

However, this qualified Real Madrid for the UEFA Cup – established in 1971 and reconstituted in 2009 as the Europa League – for which the old Fairs Cup was the forerunner. They were embarrassingly eliminated in the second round, on the away goals rule, by PSV Eindhoven. The one-time 'kings of Europe' were now finding that the quality of European teams was fast improving and hence progress in European competitions was becoming more difficult.

Real again experienced European defeat when, as Liga champions, they reached the semi-final of the 1972/73 European Cup. Although they had a relatively easy time in reaching this stage, they found themselves drawn against the 'total footballers' of Ajax, winners the previous year and, under the on-pitch direction of the brilliant Johan Cruyff, probably the world's most exciting club side. A 2-1 defeat in Holland, followed by a 1-0 loss at the Bernabéu, ensured Ajax's passage to the final. However, there was little shame attached to Real's performance, as they had been outclassed in both games. As Santillana remarked after the game, 'we lost to a special side'.

This was not one of Real Madrid's best seasons, as they finished fourth in La Liga and were knocked out of the Copa by Sporting Gijón. For the first time in 14 years, shouts of 'Muñoz Fuera' (Muñoz Out) were coming from sections of the Real support. And next season, 1973/74, would be no better.

Born in Spain?

At the 1962 World Cup finals in Chile, the Spanish national team contained several players – including Real's Santamaria (Uruguay) and Puskás (Hungary) – who had not been born in Spain, for which they were criticised in the national press. Also, Spain fell at the first hurdle, finishing bottom of their group and trailing Brazil, Mexico and Czechoslovakia.

After the country's ignominious exit from Chile, the Spanish football authorities decided to encourage the development of Spanish-born footballers. Therefore, they banned all Spanish professional clubs from acquiring and playing non-native 'foreigners', on the basis that Spaniards would assume these positions and thereby enhance Spain's international reputation. An exception was made for *oriundos*: players who were born elsewhere but could claim strong, familial, Spanish roots.

The larger clubs, such as Real and Barcelona, with their mainly Latin American imports, protested but there was little that they could do to repeal this decision, so they adopted other means of acquiring foreign players. By various means such as altering birth records and work permits, non-native players were encouraged to claim wrongly that their grandparents had been born in remote Spanish pueblos. These grounds for eligibility were not properly investigated in many cases, but the influx of incomers was slowed nonetheless.

Finally, in 1973 Barcelona – who were attempting to sign Dutch-born Johan Cruyff – hired investigators who revealed that over 60 per cent of existing oriundos had 'doctored' work permits. In May of that year, the ban was lifted. Thereafter, all clubs were permitted to sign up to two foreign players.

Over that summer, Barcelona signed Cruyff, and Real acquired Günther Netzer, a German international midfielder from Borussia Mönchengladbach. Little had changed apart from the law, which hadn't properly worked, anyway.

Bad season for Real

Netzer was 1973's 'star' signing for Real, but he did little to improve matters in La Liga as they ended in eighth position, their lowest since the disastrous season of 1947/48. Also, in Round 1 of the UEFA Cup, Real were eliminated by the virtually unknown English club Ipswich Town, who led 1-0 after the first leg at Portman Road and held Real to a goalless draw at the Bernabéu.

Netzer found it difficult to fit into Real's fast, free-flowing tactics, as – although as creative as the others in the team – he played in a casual manner but more slowly. He remained in Spain for only two more seasons. However, other German international players were soon to head south to Madrid.

A more important factor in Real's current misfortunes was the departure of their manager Miguel Muñoz, who had been in the position for the previous 14 years and had also captained the team. He was replaced, on a caretaking basis, by Luis Molowny, who had joined the club in the same year as Muñoz. The displeasure expressed towards the manager by the members had finally forced the Real board to act. Muñoz was, and remains to this day, Real's longest-serving manager.

Cruyff inspires Barcelona

Only one month after Molowny assumed control of Real, Barcelona travelled to the Bernabéu for a Liga match. That day – 17 February 1974 – the Catalan side, led majestically by Cruyff, inflicted one of Real's greatest humiliations: a 5-0 defeat at the Bernabéu.

When Cruyff had eventually made his debut appearance for his new club, Barcelona were fourth from the bottom of Primera. Inspired by Cruyff at his best, they embarked on a 22-game unbeaten run and won La Liga, ten points ahead of second-placed Atlético and 16 in front of Real.

In the February game at the Bernabéu, they tore Real apart, outclassing them in every department. This was, at the least, revenge for the 11-1 game, and it was organised and run by Cruyff. Spanish national newspapers, even Real's 'house organ' *Marca*, asked after the match if this was the game which marked the ultimate decline of Real, such was the Catalan side's superiority.

Real did beat Barcelona 4-0 in the final of the Copa in June that year, but Cruyff and Netzer were absent, both preparing for the World Cup. Also, foreign players were not permitted to play in the Copa. So, it really was not the definitive payback which Real – still reeling from the February humbling – were desperately seeking. There was little doubt that Cruyff and Barcelona had been the top team of that season in Spain.

Real under pressure

As the 1974/75 Liga kicked off, Molowny had given way to a new Real Madrid manager. Miljan Miljanic arrived from Red Star Belgrade. He was a noted tough guy who emphasised team discipline and adopted more defensive tactics than had previous Real managers.

He brought in Paul Breitner, the university-educated Maoist from Bayern Munich, who was to play alongside Netzer in a midfield role. Also, from the youth team, came José Antonio Camacho, who established himself as essential in central defence. Real ended the season by winning La Liga 12 points ahead of second-placed Zaragoza. They claimed the doblete by beating Atlético in the final on penalties, the first time in Spain that penalties had been used to decide such a game.

Many supporters at the Bernabéu objected to Miljanic's 4-3-3, defensive, long-ball game which was not Real's style. But it achieved results when the previous 'possession game' was not succeeding.

The fact that Real were beaten 2-1 on aggregate by Tenerife, from Segunda, in the following season's Copa was a source of some embarrassment. But, as compensation, the Madrid side did win La Liga again in 1975/76.

Real encounter Derby

In 1975/76, Real were also back in the European Cup. Having eliminated Dynamo Bucharest, they met Derby County at the Baseball Ground in the first leg of Round 2 on 22 October 1975.

Brian Clough, who had guided Derby to their first-ever English Division One title in 1972, had typically fallen out with the club and left in 1973. He was replaced by Scottish ex-player Dave Mackay. Mackay had won the First Division title in 1974/75, for the club's second and final time, and he retained a fast, attacking side. Striker Charlie George had joined Derby County from Arsenal, for whom he had scored the winner in the 1971 FA Cup final. George scored a hat-trick against Real, and Derby won by a completely unexpected 4-1, a result which stunned but delighted the home fans.

At the Bernabéu, however, Real Madrid – masters of the *remontada* (comeback) – had equalised on aggregate by full-time, with Santillana claiming two. Derby, without their talismanic Bruce Rioch and Franny Lee, were on the ropes, and Santillana scored the winner and completed his own hat-trick in extra time to eliminate a tired and chastened Derby.

A Santillana equaliser in Madrid against Borussia Mönchengladbach, after a 2-2 draw in Germany, sent Real to the semi-final against Bayern Munich, who held Real to 1-1 in Spain. A brace from Müller in Germany, with no reply from

Real, meant the Madrid team were again out of Europe. Bayern went on to lift their third European Cup in succession.

In the next season, 1976/77, Real collapsed. They conceded 53 goals to finish ninth in La Liga and were knocked out of the European Cup in Round 2 by Bruges. It came as little surprise to the increasingly disgruntled fans when Miljanic was fired and Molowny returned as caretaker manager.

Franco's death

'How can they tell?' was Dorothy Parker's response when she was informed about the death of ex-US President Calvin Coolidge.

When Franco died on 20 November 1975, the reactions within Spain ranged from the sorrowful to the celebratory, but there were few people who responded to the news with Parker's witty flippancy. The dictator's death was regarded by many Spaniards as one of the most important events in Spain that century, and they treated it as such.

However, although Franco and his regime had continued to pursue their dictatorial policies, Spain had been gradually evolving since the 1960s into a more liberal and tolerant society, and many had been planning for the post-Franco era. This liberal expansionism had been generated by the economic 'boom' of the 1960s, itself largely caused by the unprecedented success of mass tourism, the greater political ties with Europe, and the abandonment of economic autarky, all of which facilitated the signing of the country's 1970 trade agreement with the European Community.

Accompanying these motive factors were a decline in Spain's reliance on agriculture, a corresponding increase in emigration to the cities where industrial work was plentiful, investment in infrastructure, a growing literacy rate, and a general sense of the need for electoral and democratic reform.

Francoism's many opponents, principally the Communist Party, had moved from *rupturista* (struggle from without) to *aperturtista* (change from within), although the Basque Country's Basque Euskadi Ta Askatasuna (Basque Homeland and Liberty [ETA]) continued its policy of armed violence for a further 30 years.

Other spheres of anti-Francoist unrest included: the burgeoning, educated, professional middle classes; the growing number of active political dissenters; the trades unions; the younger clerics in the Roman Catholic Church (an institution whose power was waning); and many others in the Spanish population who were insisting on change.

Madrilian newspapers with news of Franco's death, 19 November 1975.

'Time for change'

King Juan Carlos had been appointed by Franco as successor to El Caudillo. On Franco's death, and despite the critics who perceived this handover as 'more of the same', Juan Carlos assumed the role of constitutional monarch.

Although he had tearfully announced Franco's death, Carlos got straight down to business. He appointed Adolfo Suárez as the interim prime minister, legalised the Communist Party and oversaw the formation of a coalition of left and right to form a government based in Madrid. The controversial Pacto de Olvido (Amnesty Act) – 'national reconciliation' through the forgetting and forgiving of previous war crimes – was passed by the Cortes (national assembly) after the 1978 General Election, the first to be held in 42 years.

In 1978, the new Constitution was enacted. This declared universal suffrage, a two-chamber elected Cortes, and the division of Spain into 17 'quasi-federal' communities which were importantly to remain as part of the Spanish state. Crucially, there was to be 'no state religion'.

The February 1982 General Election was a landmark in modern Spanish history. The original coalition splintered, then collapsed, and an 80 per cent voter turn-out elected the left-reformist Partido Socialista Obrero Español (Spanish Socialist Workers' Party [PSOE]), led by Felipe González, which had campaigned under the slogan 'Por el cambio' (Time for change).

The PSOE was to govern Spain for the following 14 years. At a profound and bloody cost, democracy had finally been achieved in Spain.

King Juan Carlos I, standing up in an open car as he is driven through Madrid after his proclamation, 22 November, 1975. *AP*

Real Madrid again top La Liga

Günter Netzer left Real Madrid before La Liga season 1977/78 kicked off. Also absent that season was right-winger Amancio, who retired from playing after 14 years' service at the club. He joined Real's technical staff to look after the youth team, and he was the man who nurtured the next superstar generation, the 'Quinta'.

The new arrivals included the fiery Juan Gómez ('Juanito') from Burgos, and Ulrich ('Uli') Stielike from Borussia. A goalscoring forward, Juanito replaced Amancio, and he made almost 300 appearances for the club. A car accident, as he was walking home from watching a Real home match, claimed his life in 1992. Stielike was a German-international central midfielder/sweeper who was to play alongside Camacho in defence.

Real were beaten 3-2 in the Copa by a fast-improving Real Sociedad side, but they reclaimed La Liga, ending six points ahead of Barcelona and with Santillana scoring 24 Liga goals. Although they were not in Europe that season, the newcomers fitted well into the Real squad, and life was looking rosier for the Madridismos. However, shortly after the season's end, Spanish football and particularly Real Madrid were shocked by the death of Santiago Bernabéu.

59

Death of Santiago Bernabéu

The man who is generally credited with having transformed Real Madrid into one of the world's most successful football clubs, Bernabéu died from cancer on 2 June 1978 at the age of 82. He had been associated with Real for almost 70 years: as a 14-year-old junior inside-forward, senior player, general manager, manager and president.

He had fought alongside the Nationalists during the Civil War, but he subsequently allowed little to stand between him and Real. As president for the previous 35 years, he had presided over the winning of six European Cups and 15 Liga titles. He had received a variety of other personal and footballing honours, the most recent being the freedom of Madrid.

He was mourned by players and staff at Real. Such was the esteem in which Bernabéu was held, at the 1978 World Cup finals in Argentina, FIFA held a three-day mourning period to commemorate his life.

However, Real had to cope and make speedy changes. Within 19 days of his departure, the members had elected 71-year-old Luis de Carlos as the club's new president. The new man was to assume control with immediate effect, and this cautious but canny president remained in the role until 1985.

La Liga titles keep coming

Real won La Liga in both 1978/79 and 1979/80 and therefore remained in the following seasons' European Cups. However, in the first season, they were humiliated by a Round 2 defeat by Grasshoppers Zurich, the Swiss winning 2-0 in the second leg at home and going through on away goals. Zurich departed the tournament in the following round, losing to the eventual surprise competition winners Nottingham Forest.

In 1979/80, Real reached the semi-final and cruised to a 2-0 win at the Bernabéu over one of Germany's oldest clubs, Hamburg. But they crumbled disastrously away from home, succumbed 5-1, and were out. With new manager Vujadin Boskov having taken over from Molowny, and fielding English winger Laurie Cunningham, Real claimed their third doblete in 1979/80 with a 2-0 defeat of Valencia in the Copa final.

These Liga titles were to be the last for five years as, although Real remained contenders, other teams – including, but not only, Atlético Madrid and Barcelona – were rediscovering their talent, capabilities and ambition. In particular, the Basque Country – in the shape of Real Sociedad and Athletic Bilbao – were experiencing a footballing revival, and Real were taking a back seat. But by the mid-1980s, Real would be back, and back in some style.

A European Cup final . . . at last

One legacy of Bernabéu's reign for Real's president de Carlos was a series of financial problems, so no new, high-level, expensive players entered the Bernabéu's gates in 1980/81.

His Real team spent much of the season around mid-table, but a late spurt moved them upwards. Although Real won their final game, a late goal conceded by Sporting de Gijón that day gave victory to Real Sociedad, who narrowly won their first-ever La Liga title, with Real Madrid in second place. Sporting Gijón again spoilt the party when they eliminated the Madrid boys from the Copa by 4-3 in the quarter-final.

Both major domestic titles had eluded Real, but the European Cup, the competition in which they had continually disappointed since their 1966 triumph, was also on the Real agenda that season. Surely this time . . . ?

'When Irish Eyes Are Smiling'

¿Dónde es Limerick? (Where is Limerick?) was a question posed by the players at the Bernabéu Stadium after the first-round draw in the 1980/81 European Cup. And, aside from Laurie Cunningham, probably very few, if any, of them had heard of the place.

A town of around 70,000 inhabitants and located in south-west Ireland at the mouth of the River Shannon, Limerick had clinched the second League of Ireland title in their 42-year history. They were now to meet mighty Real in the opening games of the European Cup. Only five members of the team had ever played in Europe, and the wages of the Real first team were over 50 times greater than the entire Limerick staff. But Limerick were run by player/manager Eoin Hand, an Irish ex-international defender, and were certainly up for the encounter. This was despite the fact that Real had recently beaten Athletic Bilbao 7-1 and considered Limerick mere minnows.

The first leg was held at Dublin's Lansdowne Road ground, as Limerick's Markets Field stadium was considered too small for the expected crowd. In the event, only just over 6,000 spectators turned up in Dublin, in a ground which could easily accommodate five times that number. The Irish side had a small fan base, but that was not apparent from the determined way they began the game.

By half-time, Limerick had had a 'goal' ruled offside in the opening minute, were running the Real defence ragged and were 1-0 ahead of their illustrious competitors. With only 20 minutes remaining, substitute Pineda dived in the box, a penalty was controversially awarded, and Juanito equalised from the spot. In the 85th minute, a Pineda shot was deflected past the Irish keeper, and a much relieved Real snatched a 2-1 victory. At home in the Bernabéu, in front of 60,000 fans (of whom around 100 had made the trip from Ireland), Real secured their progress with a 5-1 win. Phew!

Real had learnt that it is always unwise to underestimate the capacity of one's lowlier opponents to inflict, albeit briefly, serious damage to one's lofty reputation. They had, however, forgotten this lesson almost 30 years later when they played Alcorcón in the Copa del Rey . . . .

Limerick United go 1-0 ahead at Lansdowne Road. *Alamy*

From Limerick to Liverpool

After the torrid time Real had of it in Dublin, Round 2 was something of a breeze when they defeated Honved 3-0. The quarter-final (Spartak Moscow beaten 3-2) was a tighter game, and, in the semi-final against old enemy Inter Milan, the 2-0 result (goals by Santillana and Juanito) in Spain was sufficient to defeat Inter on aggregate, although Inter won the second leg 1-0 in a tense encounter.

Real had reached their first European Cup final for 15 years and were looking for their seventh trophy, while Liverpool were seeking their third. The final – played on 27 May 1981 at Paris's Parc des Princes stadium – promised a feast of exciting football in a closely fought match. Real had fast, talented forwards, such as Juanito, Cunningham and Santillana, backed up by Camacho, Del Bosque and Stielike. Liverpool had the Scottish central unit of Hansen, Souness and Dalglish. It was also a contrast between the managers, with Boskov's attacking flair ranged against Bob Paisley's disciplined efficiency.

However, the game developed into a bad-tempered, dull and defensive contest, enlivened only by left-back Alan Kennedy's angled, close-range goal in the 82nd minute. Real had eight minutes in which to equalise, and they couldn't. Boskov complained of Liverpool's 'machine-like' performance, and Paisley confessed that his team had been poor. But they had won the European Cup.

Real had once again missed out on the increasingly elusive trophy, and it was to take them another six years before they were able to re-enter the tournament.

Alan Kennedy scores the winner for Liverpool. *Marca*

'Madrid de Los Garcia'

The main reasons for Real's prolonged absence from Europe's prime tournament lay first in the Basque Country, specifically in Bilbao and San Sebastián, and then in Catalonia.

In 1981/82, Real Madrid suffered, by their standards, another disappointing season. Club president de Carlos remained concerned about Real's financial situation, and again no 'big names' arrived in Madrid. In La Liga, the team trailed the usual suspects, but by January 1982 they briefly led Primera. They then had an unhappy run of six games without a win and ended the season in third spot. Real Sociedad, the team of the moment, retained the trophy, three points ahead of the Madridismos.

In the UEFA Cup in March 1982, there was little sign of a remontada, as Real were coshed by Kaiserlautern 5-0 in the second leg of the quarter-final and so exited the 'second-tier' European tournament. The only trophy collected by Real was the Copa, when they beat Sporting Gijón in the final. This meant they were again in Europe the next season, albeit in the 'third-tier' Cup Winners' Cup.

This season, incidentally, was known at the Bernabéu as the final year of 'Madrid de Los Garcia'. The reason? Between 1978 and 1982, Real had no fewer than seven players registered with the name 'Garcia'. A shame it wasn't Puskás.

Another final lost

In the following season, 1982/83, the legendary Alfredo Di Stéfano returned to the Bernabéu as head coach, but still Real could not shake off their unaccustomed role of 'second-best'. In La Liga, they ended one point behind Athletic Bilbao, and the Copa final against Diego Maradona's Barcelona was decided by a last-minute diving header from the Catalan club's Marcos Alonso.

They also reached the Cup Winners' Cup final, surviving in the later stages of the tournament against Inter Milan and Austria Vienna to meet Alex Ferguson's Aberdeen on a wet and muddy pitch in Gothenburg on 11 May 1983. The Dons took a seventh-minute lead, but Juanito quickly equalised from the penalty spot. The score remained level until extra time, when, with eight minutes to play, a glancing header from substitute John Hewitt secured Aberdeen's first and only European trophy.

The supremacy which Real Madrid had assumed throughout the 1970s was now coming under threat, and life was bleak at the Bernabéu. However, this was all to change within a couple of years. By the middle of the decade, Real were to recapture their dominance as one of Spain and Europe's great sides, as the talents of their Madrid-born, youthful reserve players came to the fore.

Casillas: the Real Madrid cradle

One of the unusual features of La Liga is that a club's reserve team is permitted to field a side in the same league system. However, they are not permitted to share a division. So, if a club is relegated from Primera to Segunda, and if its 'B' team is already there, then the latter must step down to a lower division. Likewise, if the club inhabits Primera and its reserves win Segunda, the 'B' team stays where it is.

This latter event occurred at the end of the 1982/83 season when Casillas – the Real 'B' team, and the best reserve side in Spain – found itself at the top of Segunda. Although during the following season Casillas stayed in the lower division, several of its players gradually moved up to the first team. These were virtually all Madrid-born young lads, products of La Fábrica (the club's youth academy or cantera) who had been coached by Amancio Amaro.

Despite the absorption of these younger players into the senior side, Real's 1983/84 season continued much as before. A 6-2 away defeat by Málaga in their second game and their elimination by Sparta Prague in Round 1 of the UEFA Cup did not augur well for the season. Real finished a close second to Athletic Bilbao in La Liga, and a penalty shoot-out in the Copa semi-final also went in favour of the Basque club. Di Stéfano was fired, and his role was taken by caretaker Molowny, but a footballing revolution was underway at the Bernabéu.

'A change is gonna come'

In the late 1970s and early 1980s, in the heady years of post-Francoism and the promise offered by the 1982 election of the Socialist Party, Madrid embraced a sociocultural counter-revolution: La Movida Madrileña.

La Movida was a hedonistic celebration of the new sense of freedom, democracy and liberalism, explored through film, art, literature, music and much else, and was joyfully paraded under the words 'Solo se viva una fez' ('You only live once'). The repression and grimness of the dictatorship years were overtaken in Madrid by an explosion of self-expression, creativity and radical, artistic experimentation.

In November 1983, an article had appeared in *El Pais* in which the author, Julio César Iglesias, hailed Amancio's coaching of Casillas and, especially, five of his young players. In his piece, Iglesias described them as the 'Quinta del Buitre' ('Vulture Squad'), a phrase which has, over time, entered the mythology of Spanish football.

The Quinta can be seen as the footballing reflection of La Movida. With their inventive imagination and flair for the unexpected, this new generation of innovative footballers was at the core of the team which dominated Spanish football in the second half of the 1980s.

Who were the Quinta?

Amancio and Di Stéfano, before the latter abruptly left the club for the second time, were the principal conduits for the Quinta into the Real Madrid senior team.

Shortly after the laudatory *El Pais* article, sweeper/centre-back Manuel Sanchís and technically gifted midfielder Martin Vázquez were promoted. These two were followed by the goalscoring front man Emilio Butragueño and speedy striker Miguel Pardeza (the only member not from Madrid). José González ('Michel') arrived in the first team early in season 1984/85, and the Quinta were then complete. Their quietly charismatic leader Butragueño, who often appeared unspectacular but was deadly in front of goal, was nicknamed 'El Buitre' (the Vulture), hence the name of the quintet.

The Quinta were versatile, skilful, fast and, to a degree, mutually codependent. In this sense, they were reminiscent of the 'habit football' of the Celtic side of the late 1960s and the all-conquering early-1970s Ajax. Their apparent nonchalance concealed a fierce determination, and they delighted in pressurising opponents. Their performances were a revelation to the fans at the Bernabéu.

At the start of 1984/85, Molowny acquired Argentinian striker Jorge Valdano from Zaragoza to complement the long-serving Santillana and Juanito, but the team was still settling in and managed only fifth place in La Liga, 17 points behind Barcelona. They did, however, win the UEFA Cup, beating Hungary's Videoton through *grandes remontadas* (great comebacks) at the Bernabéu against Anderlecht and Inter Milan. Butragueño's hat-trick against the Belgians in Madrid served notice of his intentions.

The members of La Quinta del Buitre: Burtragueno, Pardeza, Michel, Sanchis and Vasquez. *As*

Sánchez joins the Quinta

In May 1985, Luis de Carlos resigned, and Ramón Mendoza was voted the new president of Real Madrid. A flamboyant, outgoing character with an intriguing background (which included, said his critics, spying for the KGB), Mendoza was a sociable and charismatic wheeler-dealer.

Over that summer he acquired from neighbouring Atlético the prolific Mexican striker Hugo Sánchez, from Real Betis he brought in midfielder Rafael Gordillo, and from Sporting Gijón came centre-back Antonio Maceda. The last two were skilled defenders chosen to add physical support to the relatively lightweight forward line. Their roles prompted Sánchez to suggest that the group change their nickname to 'La Quinta de Los Machos' (the Virile Quintet).

Although some of the more staid club members might have bridled at this facile comment, Sánchez's subsequent performances in Real's white shirt ensured an end to criticism of the player. The Mexican quickly slotted in alongside the Quinta, and he proved to be one of the most prolific goalscorers in the club's history.

In the 1985/86 season, Real won their first Liga title for six years, an emphatic 11 points ahead of second-placed Barcelona. Sánchez and Butragueño were forging an almost intuitive on-pitch understanding. El Buitre was often content to supply the obsessive scorer with the final touch, although Butragueño also darted through, when required, to finish off a move. The older forwards – Santillana and Juanito – were reaching the end of their reign, and the younger pretenders were scoring the goals.

Hugo Sánchez in action against Barcelona in November 1985. *Alamy*

The Quinta reign in Spain

For the following four seasons, the Vulture Squad were unquestionably at the heart of domestic football in Spain, and Real Madrid were the dominant club side in the country.

In 1986/87, under new coach Leo Beenhakker, they again claimed La Liga and repeated the feat the next season. With Pardeza having left to join Real Zaragoza, the Quinta hit peak form in 1987/88, winning La Liga by 11 points over runners-up Real Sociedad, finishing 23 points ahead of Barcelona, and with Sánchez awarded his second successive Pichichi.

In the following season, now bolstered by German international midfield playmaker Bernd Schuster (formerly of Barcelona), Real won the doblete five points clear of the Catalans in La Liga and also defeated Valladolid in the Copa final.

In 1989/90, the Quinta had a new manager. Beenhakker had resigned after his doblete triumph, and in came John Toshack from Real Sociedad. The Welshman oversaw Real's fifth successive Liga victory. They scored a Liga-record 107 goals that season, with 38 of them coming from Sánchez, and ended their Liga run nine points ahead of Valencia in second place.

The success of these players over that five-year period was a magnificent achievement. However, for the following few years Madrid were to cede dominance to Barcelona. Despite all the trophies and plaudits they had achieved, the Quinta had not managed to win Europe's leading trophy, although they certainly tried hard enough.

Hugo Sánchez, Buyp, Parra and Schuster raise the Spanish Cup in 1988. *Alamy*

. . . and in the UEFA Cup

Real Madrid won their second consecutive UEFA Cup in 1985/86, beating Cologne 5-3 in the two-legged final. On their way, they staged two further grandes remontadas. The first was overcoming a 1-5 hammering by Borussia Mönchengladbach in Germany with a 4-0 win in Madrid, Santillana scoring two in the final 15 minutes, which ensured their quarter-final status. The second was turning a 1-3 Italian defeat by Inter into a 6-4 aggregate victory in Spain, Santillana again emerging the saviour with his two extra-time goals.

These were Real's only trophies in the competition, which changed its name in 2009 to the Europa League. The expansion of the European Cup in 1991/92 into the Champions League, and its change in format, meant that this latter tournament became Real's principal focus of interest.

...but not in the European Cup

As a result of their Liga triumphs, Real were back in the European Cup for the following five years. It had been just over 20 years since they last won the trophy, and Mendoza was determined to reclaim the ultimate prize. Despite possessing some of Europe's most valued players – among others, Sánchez, Valdano and Butragueño up front, Sanchís and Camacho in defence and Gallego in midfield – they reached three successive semi-finals but were defeated in each one.

In 1986/87, Real squeezed through against Juventus and Red Star Belgrade before meeting Bayern Munich in the penultimate games. These were both ugly, ill-tempered affairs, and Real's talent for comebacks deserted them in Madrid where a 1-0 win, amid serious crowd trouble at the Bernabéu, hardly compensated for the 4-1 battering they had suffered in Munich.

In the following season, Bayern were Real's quarter-finalists, and the Spanish side sought revenge. Two late goals from Butragueño and Sánchez saw Real bring a 3-2 defeat back to Madrid. With high crowd barriers and a massive police presence at the Bernabéu, a 2-0 defeat of the German side was sufficient to reach the semi-final where they faced Holland's PSV. Real were favourites to reach the final but, in two games which they should have won, they were kept out, mainly due to the excellence of PSV's goalie Van Breukelen. The final aggregate score was 1-1, and PSV went through on away goals.

The third semi-final was in 1989 against Arrigo Sacchi's formidable AC Milan, featuring Holland's Van Basten, Gullit and Rijkaard. Real held them 1-1 in Madrid, in front of a 95,000 crowd, but wilted at the San Siro and succumbed 5-1 to a superior side.

The 'Dream Team'

Despite their final Liga flourish in 1989/90, it was becoming clear that Real Madrid were losing their impetus in European football, a view reinforced by being knocked out in the second round of the European Cup by, again, AC Milan. There were also indications that their domestic dominance was increasingly under challenge, particularly from Barcelona.

Since his appointment as manager of the Catalan club in 1988, Cruyff had been under growing pressure from his president Josep Nuñez to deliver. He had acquired attacking sweeper Ronald Koeman and elegant midfielder Michael Laudrup from Juventus, and both were in the side which faced Real at the Mestella in April 1990 in the Copa del Rey final. Recent signing Fernardo Hierro, a tall central midfielder with an eye for goal, lined up alongside Schuster and Sanchís, with Butragueño and Sánchez the front men.

Barcelona beat Real 2-0, and this was the day the music died, at least for the Quinta. A couple of months later, Cruyff persuaded Hristo Stoichkov – 'El Pistolero' – to leave CSKA Sofia, and the manager later that year promoted young defensive midfielder 'Pep' Guardiola to the senior side. The Dutchman now had the basis of what became known as his 'Dream Team', which was to win the next four Liga titles and, in two years' time, gain Barcelona the club's first European Cup trophy.

Not Tenerife again?

In 1990/91, Barcelona won La Liga, 12 points clear of Real Madrid in third place, their first title loss in six years. This was an emphatic and deserved win for the Catalan side, but their next two Liga victories involving Real have often been described as 'lucky' and were decided on the last day of each season. Furthermore, the 'Dream Team' titles were decided by results elsewhere. In the following two seasons, Real Madrid could have won the Primera if their final Liga fixture had gone their way but, for whatever reason, they lost, and Barcelona won the title by a one-point margin.

Throughout the 1990s, Tenerife – a team more used to existence in lower divisions – were in La Liga. In June 1992, Real Madrid and Barcelona were neck-and-neck until the final game of the league season. If Real beat Tenerife away, they would be champions. By half-time, Real were 2-0 ahead and were cruising towards the title. By the end of the game, Real had conceded three soft goals, were defeated 3-2, and the players were distraught. Barcelona claimed La Liga.

In 1992/93, the perverse fixture list again paired them on the final day against the Canary Islands team. Once more, they had to win to beat Barcelona and become champions, and they flew to Tenerife with an air of foreboding. Sure enough, they lost 2-0 and for the second time handed the title to an exultant but disbelieving Barcelona.

The ultimate irony was that Tenerife were managed by Jorge Valdano who, as a player, had contributed so much to the Quinta side of the mid-to-late 1980s until ill health forced his retirement. The following season, Valdano was hired by Real as their new coach.

75

Real resume battle

Valdano's return to the Bernabéu coincided with the arrival at Real of Michael Laudrup. Laudrup had problems working with the Dutchman Cruyff at Barcelona, and the final straw at the end of the previous season was his being omitted from the club's 1994 European Cup final against AC Milan in Athens.

Barcelona's 4-0 comprehensive defeat by the Italian side marked the end of the 'Dream Team' and, at the close of that season, the sacking of Cruyff. Another newcomer was goalkeeper Santiago Cañizares from Celta Vigo, who was soon to replace long-serving Paco Buyo between the sticks.

At the season's end, Real won La Liga for the first time in five years, with Barcelona in fourth place, nine points behind Real. The order was changing again, a fact underlined by Real's 5-0 dismissal of their Catalan rivals at the Bernabéu. Chilean striker Iván Zamorano scored a hat-trick, and Laudrup was Real's outstanding playmaker in the game. Zamorano's 28 goals saw him finish the season as Liga top scorer, but he was soon to depart.

The most enduring legacy of Valdano's relatively brief period in charge – he left in January 1997 – was his promotion of 17-year-old Raúl González Blanco to the first team. The youngster had been at Atlético Madrid's youth academy until the club's chairman Jesús Gil closed it down. At this point, the gifted youngster moved to Real's academy, where his presence was welcomed. Known simply as Raúl, he was to become the heir to Butragueño.

Raúl during his first season in the Real first team. *Alamy*

76

Capello's single season

The season which followed was not a good one for Real Madrid, as they could finish in only sixth place in La Liga and were beaten 2-1 by Juventus in the new Champions League (European Cup, as was). In November, Ramón Mendoza was finally forced to resign the club presidency after incurring the blame for escalating financial problems, and his role was taken on by Lorenzo Sanz.

In December 1995, the European Court of Justice had found in favour of Jean-Marc Bosman's legal challenge against his club RC Liège. Inter alia, this overruled UEFA's prior ability to limit the number of foreigners playing for European clubs. The larger clubs had, to a degree, discovered ways around UEFA's diktat, but the 'Bosman Ruling' meant that Real were no longer legally limited to home-grown players. This had a major influence on their acquisition of non-Spaniards, as soon became evident.

In 1996/97, although this was the first season in 19 years that they hadn't qualified for Europe, they again won La Liga. Under new coach Fabio Capello, in came left wing-back Roberto Carlos, midfielders Clarence Seedorf and Fernando Redondo, and forwards Predrag Mijatović and Davor Šuker. The line-up was turning multinational.

Under Capello's guidance, Šuker scored 24 goals, and the blossoming Raúl netted 21. The manager returned to Italy at the season's end, having fallen out badly with Sanz, and he was replaced for 1997/98 by Germany's much-travelled manager Jupp Heynckes.

Roberto Carlos is 1997. *Alamy*

A disappointing Liga season

Real had not won the European Cup/Champions League for 32 long years. A string of managers and players had attempted the task and, now that Real were back in the tournament, this was Heynckes's objective: to recover the Holy Grail and bring it back to Madrid in triumph.

To assist him, he had two new players: striker Fernando Morientes and speedy midfielder Christian Karembeu. Not the most assertive of managers, and unable to exercise discipline when required, the German found it difficult to motivate his increasingly international squad, unlike Capello whose brusque demeanour irritated some of the squad. Real had an unpromising start to the season, winning just one game from their first ten in La Liga.

Although their form improved as the season wore on, at the end of what was otherwise a momentous season for the club, they ended in fourth place. They were also knocked out of the Copa del Rey in the second round by the Basque Country's Alavés, then in Segunda. However, 1998 was the year they finally ended their European Cup jinx, a feat which had been beyond the powers of the Quinta.

. . . but a European triumph

The Champions League began in 1991/92, in which year Barcelona won the trophy. Initially, it was the same format as the European Cup but with the quarter-finals replaced by two leagues. Each team played the three others in the league on a home-and-away basis, and the league winners of each group met in the final.

As the decade progressed, the league system became more complicated and inclusive, as it was essentially designed to ensure that the wealthier, prestigious European clubs were not eliminated by upstarts in the earlier stages of the tournament. The term 'Champions League' gradually became a misnomer, as clubs who had not been league winners but fulfilled certain criteria in FIFA's rating calculations and came from historically leading football countries could also enter the competition at different stages.

The last game to consist of two clubs which had reached the European Cup final by straightforward home-and-away elimination through the various knockout stages was in 1991 in Bari, when Red Star Belgrade beat Marseille in a penalty shoot-out.

Gabriel Hanot, the proposer of the original European Cup, would no doubt have been, at the very least, disappointed at what FIFA and the money men were doing with his idea.

79

Champions League, 1997/98:
La Septima

In the 1997/98 season's Champions League, Real's performance was markedly superior to that on the domestic front.

They glided fairly comfortably through the initial league stage, finishing top of their group, and met Bayer Leverkusen in the quarter-final. A draw away, then a 3-0 win in Madrid, found Real facing another German club, Borussia Dortmund, in the semi-final with the first leg in Madrid.

The game was delayed early on, after the incessant movement and frenzied jumping of the Ultra Sur fans – the extreme, right-wing Real supporters' group, based at the stadium's southern end – fractured one of the goalposts. It took 75 minutes to bring a replacement from the training ground, the Ciudad Deportiva, a mile or so up the road. Borussia wanted the game restarted, but Real declined the request and ended 2-0 winners. A goalless draw in Dortmund gave Real Madrid their first European Cup final (sorry, Champions League final) in 17 years.

The final was staged in the new Amsterdam Arena on 20 May 1998. It was Juventus's third such final in succession, but it was Real's first for 17 years, so the latter's players were about to produce their best. There were 21 internationals on the pitch at kick-off, with six on the bench, and the forward lines alone promised much: Real's Raúl, Morientes and Mijatović against

Victor Sanchez celebrates at the final whistle with
goalkeeper Bodo Illgner at the Amsterdam Arena. *Colorsport*

Juve's Del Piero, Inzaghi and Zidane. How about that for attacking power?

Juventus had the early momentum, but Real grew increasingly confident, with a half-time score of 0-0. In the 66th minute, Roberto Carlos's shot rebounded to Mijatović, and the Montenegrin striker flipped the ball at a tight angle past the Italian club's keeper. When the whistle blew for the end of the game, Real had won La Septima (the seventh), and their first European Cup for 32 years. As Juventus manager Marcello Lippi admitted, 'Real Madrid deserved to win'.

You can imagine the Madridismos' celebrations on the streets of Amsterdam and Madrid: a combination of delight and unbridled relief. Real Madrid had won back 'their' trophy.

Back to business

Lorenzo Sanz no doubt much enjoyed the triumph, but it is unlikely he shared this emotion with manager Jupp Heynckes as he fired the German manager eight days after the famous victory.

Sanz then replaced the German with Camacho (who hung on for under a month), Guus Hiddink (eight months) and John Toshack (just over a year). Under Toshack's tenure, Real bought in the young striking prodigy Nicolas Anelka from a relieved Arsenal for £23.5 million and balanced this by obtaining a substantially older but much wiser Steve McManaman on a free transfer from Liverpool.

At the end of 1998/99, Real finished second in La Liga (11 points behind Barcelona) and were dismissed 3-1 from the Champions League quarter-final by Dynamo Kiev. They were also beaten 6-0 by Valencia in the Copa del Rey, their highest-ever domestic cup thrashing. This was all despite Rául scoring 25 Liga goals and Morientes claiming 19.

However, despite their variable home form, Real were again to reach the European heights at the end of the following season.

Del Bosque takes over

But first, Real Madrid had to find a permanent manager or, at least, one who would last for significantly more than a year. Toshack was inevitably fired in November. Heynckes had warned at his own farewell speech the previous year that 'Madrid need to reflect on how many coaches they have had in recent years'. Toshack was the club's eighth manager in three years.

Vicente del Bosque was hired, and his stewardship was to become one of four years' duration. Del Bosque was not a man for the histrionic gesture or for ranting at his players, preferring instead to adopt a calm, watchful and rational approach to the game. He had spent his life at Real, he had been a long-serving and valuable midfielder between 1966 and 1984, and he had witnessed some turbulent times at the club. He had also been a co-founder of the Spanish footballers' union, was experienced at dealing with out-of-control egos on the pitch and in the boardroom and, most importantly, was admired and respected by the players. He was a good choice as manager.

By the end of the season, del Bosque had hauled Real up from near the bottom to fifth in La Liga (still seven points behind Deportivo de La Coruña), but his side were beaten in the Copa semi-final by Espanyol, who had bowed to the new era in 1995 by changing their name from Español to this Catalan-ised version. He had also brought in new players, including two more than useful defenders in right-back Michel Salgado and sweeper Ivan Helguera, and there were a few other changes.

The squad which del Bosque commanded in the 1999/2000 Champions League was a significantly different one to that which had won the competition only two years previously.

Champions League 2000: another trophy?

Real Madrid had topped their first group and qualified for the quarter-final in their second group (I did say that the tournament was becoming increasingly complicated).

They faced title-holders Manchester United in the quarter-final. At the Bernabéu they had to be content with a goalless draw. At Old Trafford, by half-time they were the stronger team but were only 1-0 ahead thanks to a Keane own goal. In the second period, Raúl added another, and two minutes later a sweet back-heel nutmeg (not easy) from Redondo led to Raúl's second goal. United pulled two back towards the end through Beckham and Scholes, but Real emerged with a 3-2 aggregate win.

Bayern Munich, Real Madrid's German rivals, were next in the semi-final. In Madrid, Real were dominant throughout the game. An early goal from Anelka and a Bayern own goal gave Real a 2-0 lead to take to Germany. Without the injured Hierro and Salgado, and although Bayern scored twice in the first half, Anelka planted a fine header into the German net, thereby ensuring that Real reached their second final in two years.

The 2000 European Cup final was played in the Stade de France on 24 May. Real's opponents were Valencia, who had beaten Lazio and Barcelona in the knockouts. This was the first

Vicente Del Bosque hugs Manuel Sanchis after
victory in the final at the Stade de France. *Colorsport*

time in the competition's history that the final featured two clubs from the same country.

Real began the game with only four players who had appeared in the final two years previously, and the team's power, speed and flamboyant artistry overwhelmed Valencia. Decked out in their black kit, they dominated the game, with McManaman particularly outstanding in midfield. Towards half-time, their pressing game and tactical superiority gave Morientes the opening goal, a well-executed header.

In the second half, McManaman crowned his tireless contribution with a splendid goal from the edge of the box, becoming the first British player to score for a Continental side in a European Cup final. Raúl finished off the game with a 70-yard solo run, a skip past his old mate and now Valencia keeper Canizares, and a flick into the net for Real's third.

Real collected the trophy in their white strips, and this side had probably never played better. They well deserved their 3-0 victory. Their eighth European Cup (La Octava) was also a tribute to their manager Vicente del Bosque.

Figo and the *cochinillo*

As Real Madrid's Luis Figo was taking a corner kick at the Camp Nou in November 2002, he ignored the bottles, coins and other detritus being hurled in his direction by Barcelona fans and sent the ball sailing into the penalty area.

It was only when he saw a freshly severed pig's head bouncing on the turf next to the corner flag that he realised the visceral hatred which many Catalan fans reserved for those they viewed as 'turncoats' from the true faith. Although Figo later made light of the bloody *cochinillo* incident, he was clearly unsettled by the episode. The attempted assault – for that's what it was – also underlined to a much wider audience the rather less than amicable fondness which many Catalans nurtured for supporters of Real Madrid and for 'their' players who had opted to join the bad guys in the capital city.

This was Figo's third season in the white strip and, although a winger, he had so far avoided taking corners, as he was nervous about getting too close to the *culés* (a nickname for Barcelona supporters). On his previous visit with Real to Camp Nou, the anti-Figo noise and chants had been deafening. He was a traitor to Barcelona.

Figo had joined Barcelona in 1995, had made 137 Liga appearances for the club alongside Rivaldo and Kluivert, was regarded as one of the world's finest forwards and was revered by the Camp Nou faithful. Then, in the summer of 2000, he joined the enemy, Real Madrid, for a fee of around £55 million.

Why did Figo leave his comfortable, well-paid Catalan adulation and 'change sides'? The reason is that the newly elected president of Real Madrid was developing a policy of acquiring for the club, on an annual basis, a genuine world footballing star, and Figo had been offered a deal he could not refuse. Luis Figo was the first *galactico* to join Real Madrid.

The galactico era: Zidane

In the summer of 2000, Florentino Pérez was voted in as president to succeed Lorenzo Sanz. Pérez was one of Spain's richest men, owned the country's largest construction company and was friendly with its most powerful businessmen and politicians. In July 2000, Alfredo Di Stéfano introduced Figo to his new supporters at the Bernabéu. By the end of that season, Figo had been instrumental in Real securing their first Liga title in four years, seven points above Deportivo de La Coruña and 17 clear of Barcelona, with the top Liga scorer again being Raúl (24) and with many of these goals supplied by Figo and Guti.

The next galactico to arrive was the French star Zinedine Zidane, who came from Juventus for a record £75 million. Although they finished third in La Liga that season, nine points behind a re-energised Valencia, Real again reached the final of the Champions League.

The previous season, Real had been eliminated from the competition at the semi-final stage by Bayern Munich, but they had their revenge in 2001/02. They beat the Germans 3-2 in the quarter-final and faced Barcelona in the semi-final. At the Camp Nou, goals by McManaman and Zidane were sufficient to render the Bernabéu match – a 1-1 draw – insignificant.

On 15 May 2002, they met Bayer Leverkusen in the final at Glasgow's Hampden Park, invoking memories of that marvellous

1960 final at the stadium. Hampden was now much reduced in capacity, with no space remaining for the 130,000 people it could contain 40 or so years previously, but it still possessed that special blend of tension and intimacy found only in the world's finest stadiums. The game was speedy and evenly balanced, with the score 1-1 as half-time approached. Then Roberto Carlos floated in a cross which was superbly volleyed home by Zidane from the edge of the box. This goal – which still makes me gasp when I recollect it, as it was an act of genius – proved to be the winner.

Three European Cups within five years more than made up for the trophy's 32-year absence from the Bernabéu.

Zinedine Zidane wheels away to celebrate scoring an astonishing goal to put Real back in the lead at Hampden Park. *Colorsport*

'Happy Birthday To You'

The year 2002 was celebrated by Real Madrid as its 100th anniversary, and various events were held throughout the year to mark this occasion. These included opening a theme park, concerts with Placido Domingo singing the club's turgid anthem, basketball matches with US superstar Magic Johnson, and a football match to round off the year with Real playing a Rest of the World XI, a game which ended in a 3-3 draw. Given that such players as Figo, Zidane, Raul and Ronaldo were playing for Real, however, it was often difficult to notice any significant difference in class between the two teams.

Real president Florentino Pérez used his not insignificant influence with Spain's football authorities to ensure that the date for the Copa del Rey final, which was to be played that year between Real and Deportivo de La Coruña at the Bernabéu Stadium, was altered to take place on 6 March 2002, the very day in 1902 that the club came into legal existence.

Pérez also instructed Real's manager, Vicente del Bosque, to give the game a significantly higher priority, in terms of player selection and team discussion, than was Real's usual habit with this tournament. The last time Real could be bothered taking this competition seriously was in 1993 when they beat Zaragoza 2-0 in the final. Indeed, in the previous season, Real were beaten in an early round of the Copa by lowly Toledo from Segunda

B (the Spanish third division). However, such was Pérez's pride in the anniversary that he was determined Real should not only defeat the upstarts from north-western Spain, but do so with style and elegance while exuding an air of nonchalant superiority. However, this is not exactly what happened.

Depor were up for it and determined to win, if only to spite Real. They were also on their best ever run in La Liga (winner and twice runner-up over the last three years) and – during that brief period – had been regarded as one of Europe's leading teams.

In the sixth minute of the Copa del Rey encounter, Deportivo's Sergio González carved his way through Real's famed defenders Hierro and Salgado to open the scoring, and star striker Diego Tristán doubled the visitors' lead by half-time. Although Raúl pulled one back in the second half, Depor held on to win 2-1 and claim the Copa del Rey at the Bernabéu. These Galicians had the temerity to defeat Real Madrid on Real's home turf on the occasion of Real's 100th birthday. Pérez was not a happy man.

The visiting fans were delighted and waved their Deportivo de La Coruña flags in the air while good-naturedly singing 'Happy Birthday To You' in the direction of the stony-faced Real president. It took Pérez over two months and the winning of the European Cup to obliterate the humiliation of that day.

Ronaldo and, er, Ronaldo

It is common for non-football fans to confuse Ronaldo Luís Nazário de Lima with Cristiano Ronaldo dos Santos Aveiro, as both were known on the pitch as 'Ronaldo', both were internationally praised goalscoring forwards and both played for Real in the early years of the 21st century. However, they were very different people.

The former was a Brazilian striker who arrived at Real from Inter Milan in 2002, scored over 100 goals for the club, and joined AC Milan in the winter of 2006. The latter is a Portuguese winger-cum-striker who joined Real in 2009, scored over 300 goals, left for Juventus in 2018, and will shortly become part of this story. During their careers, both players have received numerous awards for their almost unparalleled talents at the game of football, at club and international levels.

The Brazilian Ronaldo – widely known as 'The Phenomenon' – left Brazil in 1994 and has played for PSV, Barcelona, Inter Milan, Real Madrid and AC Milan, having scored almost 230 club goals before returning to Brazil. He is currently majority shareholder at Real Valladolid. The Portuguese Ronaldo joined Manchester United as an 18-year-old from his home country in 2003, moved to Real Madrid in 2009, then Juventus and, in 2021, returned to Manchester United. He has 189 caps for Portugal, for whom he has claimed 117 goals.

Both Ronaldos have proven themselves a pleasure to watch on the football field, and they share the status of being two of the finest footballers of their generation. Had Santiago Bernabéu still been alive, it would no doubt have gladdened his heart to see players of such ability grace his stadium.

The two Ronaldos. *Colorsport*

How could the club afford it?

These galacticos were not cheap. To date, Real, who were already in a financially tricky situation and almost £300 million in debt, had spent well over £100 million on these new players, and there were other large payments pending. Where did they find the money? President Pérez certainly had his critics, but few questioned his financial nous and ability to generate income when his club were up against it. So, Pérez considered his options.

Ciudad Deportivo, then on the outskirts of Madrid, was completed in 1963 by Santiago Bernabéu. Although owned by Real, since then the area had been a legally protected, green sports ground, containing training pitches, swimming pools, tennis courts and other recreational space for the benefit of players and club members.

By the late 20th century, it was no longer on the city outskirts, with Madrid's expansion having brought the site into the Castellana district, which was the city's financial hub, making Ciudad potentially valuable for commercial development.

With the assistance of his many contacts in the Partido Popular, who ran Madrid city council, Pérez managed to re-zone the land as fit for commercial development, and he sold the space for around £450 million, a sum which was sufficient to pay off Real Madrid's debts. This still left the club with enough funds to establish another training ground at Valdebebas, near the city airport. The new site is ten times larger than the original and also contains the Alfredo Di Stéfano stadium where Real's reserve team Castilla play their home matches.

La Liga again

The Brazilian Ronaldo – Pérez's annual galactico – came to Real in 2002 and, in his first season, scored 23 goals in del Bosque's recapture of La Liga title, achieved after a late-season 3-1 defeat of Athletic Bilbao.

However, Real were beaten by Juventus in the semi-final of that season's Champions League and were knocked out of the Copa del Rey after a 5-1 defeat by Real Mallorca. Despite their league success, Pérez displayed an increasingly irrational and self-defeating aspect of his character when he fired the manager Vicente del Bosque.

Bearing in mind his long career as a Real player, and his four-year managerial stewardship during which he had won two Liga titles and two European Cups, del Bosque certainly did not deserve such treatment. Pérez had never cared for del Bosque's retiring personality nor for his quiet but determined demeanour, and had always considered the manager insufficiently 'modern' in appearance and outlook to continue in charge of his glittering new Real. He replaced him with Carlos Queiroz, a man more attuned to contemporary marketing mores.

There were also several players whom Pérez believed not to be representative of the club's contemporary image. He had already got rid of Redondo, and out too went club captain Hierro (14 years at the club, five Ligas and three European Cups), pivotal defensive midfielder Claude Makélélé, Morientes, McManaman and others; a sign that the president was fed up with 'ordinary players'.

To underline this change in attitude, in came David Beckham.

Beckham: the decline of galacticos

In the 1990s, David 'Goldenballs' Beckham had been an essential part of the successful Manchester United side, drawn mainly from the club's youth team nurtured by Alex Ferguson and known as 'Fergie's Fledglings'.

Beckham was a marketing man's dream: a seemingly bashful, grinning, unassuming, young working-class Londoner, though immensely wealthy; a famous, highly regarded midfielder and renowned dead-ball specialist; a regular in the England national team; and happily married to 'Posh Spice', a member of the fun-tastic, all-female, pop sensation of the time, the Spice Girls.

When he arrived at Real on a £35 million transfer from Old Trafford, he was introduced by Alfredo Di Stéfano at a press conference which contained 500 selected journalists from 25 countries. He was then whisked off by the club on an 18-day tour of south-east Asia to play against such footballing giants as FC Tokyo and a Hong Kong Select XI. The point of the tour – although ostensibly to promote Beckham to his fans – was to sell Beckham merchandise. Real came home, just before the start of the 2003/04 Liga, having secured a £10 million profit from the tour.

It is little surprise that several of Real's players were less envious of than incredulous at the attention paid by Real to Beckham, certainly in comparison to the club's treatment of them as 'only footballers' and not galacticos. They were also exhausted by the number of pre-season games they had played, the constant attention they had to pay to their fans, as well as by acting as cannon-fodder for the latest galactico. Pérez's galactico policy, which began with Figo, was coming under increasing scrutiny, particularly as Beckham appeared to lack, during the following season, the skills necessary to adjust to the team. Even *Marca* magazine described him as 'Forrest Gump'.

Real were not to win a major trophy for the following three seasons.

Real Madrid's new signing, England's David Beckham, waves to hundreds of fans who had gathered to greet him as he paraded in his new strip in Madrid 2 July 2003. *Alamy*

A trophy drought for Real

Many external observers, such as the influential magazine *Sports Illustrated*, suggested that the Asian trip was more of an exercise in marketing the club than it was about pre-season training.

Even Figo and Zidane, team men both, criticised the galactico policy as alienating their fellow players and creating disharmony within the club. They lamented what they felt was the unnecessary and damaging departure of Makélélé. As Zidane remarked, 'The normal rule is: Never change a winning team.' This disheartened mood was obvious during 2003/04, as Real, by their standards, struggled on the pitch.

They won the first El Clásico in December, but were beaten in April by Barcelona at the Bernabéu and lost their last four Liga matches. They ended the season in fourth place, behind Deportivo, Barcelona and Valencia. They also lost the Copa final to Real Zaragoza after extra time and they were knocked out of the Champions League quarter-final by Monaco, despite Ronaldo scoring 30 goals over the season.

The following season, striker Michael Owen arrived from Liverpool, although Ronaldo remained top scorer. Over 2004/05, Real employed four separate managers, but they could finish in only second spot in La Liga. They were eliminated by Valladolid in the last-16 round of the Copa and by Juventus in the quarter-final of the Champions League. A disaffected Luis

Figo left the club in mid-season for Inter Milan.

Things did not improve in 2005/06, although they did make a wise long-term acquisition in buying the promising 19-year-old central defender Sergio Ramos from Sevilla. In La Liga, Real again occupied the second slot, albeit 12 points adrift from a newly rampant Barcelona. They were taken apart in the Copa semi-final, losing 6-1 away to Real Zaragoza, before clawing back four goals at the Bernabéu for a more dignified 6-5 defeat.

In the 2006 Champions League last-16 round, Arsenal became the first British team to defeat Real at the Bernabéu, winning 1-0 from a Thierry Henry goal, and a 0-0 draw in London bade farewell to Real from the tournament. The fact that Ronaldo was Real Madrid's top scorer that season with only 14 goals illustrates Real's problem. But again, life was about to improve.

A Ruud awakening

In February 2006, with Real trailing Barcelona by ten points, Pérez had had enough and resigned the presidency of Real.

The new president was Ramón Calderón, and he appointed Fabio Capello as manager for 2006/07. Capello had fallen out with several players and president Lorenzo Sanz during his previous spell at the club in 1996/97 and was fired after one year although he had won back La Liga title with his preferred defensive style.

As a result of Capello's return, there was a good deal of change in Real's dressing room before 2006/07 began. From Juventus came defensive-minded Fabio Cannavaro and Emerson, along with striker Ruud van Nistelrooy (Manchester United) and winger José Antonio Reyes (Arsenal). Zidane retired at the end of the previous season, while Ronaldo joined AC Milan in December 2006. There were plenty of other comings and goings.

Real finally won La Liga, on equal points with Barcelona but with a better head-to-head goal difference. However, they again toiled in the Champions League and Copa del Rey, beaten in the last-16 round in both competitions. However, van Nistelrooy's 33 goals in all competitions (25 in La Liga) were indications of the Dutchman's goalscoring potential.

But again, the inevitable happened. Capello's authoritarian manner had made him the enemy of several players, notably

Beckham, and the Italian again received the order of the boot after only one season.

Ruud van Nistelrooy rounds Steaua Bucuresti's goalkeeper Cornel Cernea in 2006. *Alamy*

Schuster et al.

It's often difficult to keep up with Real Madrid, and the nonchalant ease with which they hire and fire managers. It must be particularly difficult for the players. Still, some of the top players are handsomely rewarded and they stick around. Or they pay no attention to the merry-go-round.

However, Beckham happily moved on to the equally rewarding LA Galaxy, Roberto Carlos went to Fenerbahce at the end of 2006/07, and several others moved club when Bernd Schuster took over. Other top players – such as winger Arjen Robben and Pepe – arrived.

Under the German ex-Real midfielder, Real won La Liga, eight points ahead of Villarreal (for a change). Barcelona were third, 18 points behind the Madridismos, and Schuster's side emphasised the gap by stuffing Barcelona 4-1 in May. However, Real proceeded no further than the last 16 in the Copa and Champions League. The top scorer with 23 goals was Raúl, still slotting them in after all these years, and van Nistelrooy added a useful 20.

Schuster left the club the following season, in December 2008, and Juande Ramos took over as coach. Under Ramos, Real won 16 of the 17 games they played between the Clásicos, and he was still present when Real scrambled second place in La Liga (nine points behind Barcelona). But his side were defeated 4-1 by Liverpool in the Champions League and, even worse, were kicked out at the last-32 stage of the Copa by the unheralded Real Unión with an aggregate 6-5 score.

Everything was fairly listless at this point, until yet another manager arrived for 2009/10. Manuel Pellegrini lifted the new managerial gauntlet, which was placed in his hand by a returning president who had left the Bernabéu only two-and-a-half years previously. Florentino Pérez had returned. He and Pellegrini brought with them, for this coming season, some fine players including Cristiano Ronaldo (Manchester United), Kaká (AC Milan), Xabi Alonso (Liverpool) and Karim Benzema (Lyon).

Although Real again ended runners-up to Barcelona in season 2009/10, they won no major trophies. This season can best be summed up by a salutary match early in the season in which the Madridismo world turned upside down, and which was an experience about which all at Real Madrid will not thank you for reminding them.

'Alcorconazo'

On the evening of 27 October 2009, Real travelled across the city to play a small suburban team, AD Alcorcón, in the first leg of the fourth round (or 'round of 32') of the annual Copa del Rey.

Alcorcón were then in Segunda Division B (the third tier of the league). Although major new signings Cristiano Ronaldo and Kaká were not in the squad, Real's team that night contained internationals from seven countries – Argentina, France, Germany, Holland, Mali, Poland and Spain – while Alcorcón had only one non-Spanish player.

The annual salary of the average Alcorcón player was less than what Cristiano Ronaldo picked up in one day, while Segunda B's total annual wage bill was around one-hundredth that of Real Madrid's. Furthermore, Real's youth team played in the same division as Alcorcón, and the Real youngsters had lost only one of their previous seven matches against them. The suburban club's stadium – Estadio Santo Domingo – had a maximum capacity of 5,000, in contrast to the Bernabéu's 80,000-plus. And so on.

It was clearly going to be a walkover for Real, particularly as their team contained, among others, Diarra, Guti, Esteban ('El Pirata'), Raúl, Benzema, van der Vaart, Marcelo and van Nistelrooy. However, it was far from that, and Madrid's performance that evening was among the most embarrassing capitulations in their recent history.

In front of a 3,000 crowd, Alcorcón had three shots at goal in the first two minutes, were 3-0 ahead of a disintegrating Real by half-time, and won the game 4-0. In the second leg at the Bernabéu, Real managed to pull back one late goal and, unbelievably, they were out of the tournament, defeated 4-1.

The day after the first leg, the 4-0 result was headline news across Europe, *El Pais* coining the term 'Alcorconazo' to describe the shame felt by Real Madrid. *Marca* called it a 'historic disgrace', and the switchboard at the Bernabéu was jammed with calls demanding Pellegrini's head.

Since the end of that season, Alcorcón have been permanent members of Segunda (second tier), perhaps buoyed by their wholly unexpected toppling of the Spanish footballing giants in that match. Also, that Christmas, the most popular number in the national lottery was 27109, or 27 October 2009. Let's hope that someone won, as Real certainly did not.

'The Special One'

It will come as no surprise to discover that Pérez fired Pellegrini at the end of 2009/10. In May, before season 2010/11 began, the president appointed José Mourinho from Inter Milan as his new manager, describing the self-appointed 'Special One' as another galáctico.

Mourinho was Real Madrid's 11th coach in seven years. Before the Italian club, he had spent a few years working as a translator/researcher for Barcelona, where he had, given his caustic nature, irritated several players and officials. He nursed a particular grievance for Pep Guardiola – who he was convinced had taken the managerial job which was meant for him – and had built up a dislike for the Catalan club. This, of course, suited Pérez.

The new manager acquired midfielders Mesut Özil and Sami Khedira, defender Ricardo Carvalho and winger Ángel Di Maria. Guti and Diarra had left, as had the long-serving Raúl who, over his 550 appearances in 16 years with Real, had scored 228 goals for the club. His presence in the white strip would be missed.

Real were second in La Liga after Barcelona and acquired one trophy – the Copa del Rey – in the Portuguese manager's first season. This was the first Copa del Rey Real had managed for 18 years, and it was made sweeter by having beaten Barcelona in the final at the end of the struggle.

José Mourinho in 2011. *Alamy*

Indeed, they confronted their sworn enemy Barcelona in El Clásico no fewer than four times within 18 days at season's end: first (16 April), in a 1-1 Liga draw; second, (20 April) in a Copa 1-0 defeat of the Catalans in the final; third (27 April) in the first leg of a Champions League semi-final at the Bernabéu, losing 2-0; and finally (3 May) in the second leg in a 1-0, but ultimately futile, win in Barcelona.

'Special' no more

By the end of 2011/12, there was a cheerier mood at the Bernabéu than had been evident in recent years. This was despite Real having been nudged out of the Copa by Barcelona, and the fact that they had – for the third season in succession – been knocked out of the convoluted Champions League at the semi-final stage, this time by their German nemesis Bayern Munich. Also, the number of players entering and leaving the club was rising to ridiculous levels. And Mourinho was still fuming at playing second fiddle to Guardiola's Catalonians.

But . . . Real had won La Liga for the first time in four years, and they had done so with distinction. Their Liga season was described in the press as 'La Liga de los Récords'.

- They had won a record 32nd Liga title.
- Their 100 points tally was a record (although not for long).
- They had scored a record 121 goals, significantly more than the Quinta's 107 in 1989/90.
- They had achieved a record 16 away wins and 32 wins overall.
- They had competed in the European Cup/Champions League for a record 15th successive year.

Also, their prolific forwards had contributed to all these, with Ronaldo scoring 60 goals, Benzema claiming 32, and Higuain netting 26. It is little wonder that there was the hint of a smirk to be seen playing on Florentino Pérez's patrician face. There had not been a great deal about which to be quietly proud in the last few years.

However, as the following season staggered to an end, Real were again second to Barcelona in La Liga (by 15 points), were beaten in the Copa final by Atlético Madrid and were knocked out of the Champions League at the semi-final stage for the third year in succession, this time by Borussia Dortmund.

Mourinho proclaimed that it was 'the worst ever season in my career'. Pérez obviously agreed with José as, shortly after 2012/13 lurched to its forgettable end, the 'Special One' left Real 'by mutual consent'. Another manager had bitten the dust.

Ancelloti and Zidane

Next up in the seemingly endless catwalk of Real Madrid managers was Carlo Ancelotti, accompanied by his assistant and Real ex-superstar 'Zizou' Zidane. At the start of 2013/14, Carlo was on his seventh club in fewer than 20 years, while Zidane, who had attended the minimum of coaching courses and had no 'badges', was deputed to look after Casillas.

In his first season, though, Carlos did well and satisfied even President Pérez. Attacking arrivals included creative midfielder Isco (Ancelotti's first signing) from Malaga and, ambitiously, winger/goalscorer Gareth Bale for a world-record £100 million from Spurs. Departures were Higuain, Kaká and Özil. Bale was to become third-top scorer (22) that season, behind Benzema (24) and, naturally, Ronaldo (51).

By early March, Real headed La Liga, but they won only one of their last four games to end equal with Barcelona on points (third-placed on head-to-head goal difference) behind winner Diego Simeone's Atlético Madrid, although they defeated Atlético 3-2 in a tense Copa semi-final. Ronaldo was injured and absent from the Copa final against Barcelona on 18 April in Valencia, where Di Maria opened for Real in the 11th minute. With the score 1-1 and five minutes remaining, Bale sealed the Copa title for Real with an outstanding solo run and goal.

It was just as close in Lisbon on 24 May. On their way to the

Portuguese capital, Real had put six past Schalke 04 in Germany, then added three more at the Bernabéu for a 9-2 walkover. Then they beat both of the previous year's finalists – Borussia Dortmund 3-2 in the last eight and Bayern Munich in the semi-final, destroying the latter 4-0 on the German team's home turf – to confront their next-door neighbours in the Champions League final.

The 'mattress makers' were 1-0 ahead during the entire second half and were about to celebrate, until the third minute of injury time when Sergio Ramos headed in the equaliser from a corner. In extra time, Real were dominant, and scorers Bale and Marcelo granted Ronaldo the honour of scoring the fourth from a 120th-minute penalty.

A pretty good season, then, for 'Los Blancos'; but President Pérez, stern headmaster that he was, insisted that they must try harder in 2014/15. 'We've just won the European Cup, sir' revealed a lack of ambition, so Ancelotti and his men continued as before or, at least, tried to. But the problem was that they didn't win anything.

Although now they had access to German international central midfielder Toni Kroos, Colombia's international World Cup star James Rodriguez, ex-Manchester United striker Jávier Hernández, and goalie Keylor Navas (replacement for Iker Casillas, Real's near-legendary keeper for the previous 16 years, who left for Porto), they didn't secure a trophy.

Real were again second in La Liga, were beaten 4-2 by Atlético in the Copa and 2-1 by Juventus in the Champions League semi-final. So near yet so far, but not near enough for Pérez, who fired Ancelotti at season's end. But the Italian would soon be back.

Benitez (briefly) and Zidane

In June 2015, Madrid-born Rafael ('Rafa') Benitez was appointed coach of Real.

Under Rafa's leadership, Real were unbeaten in their first ten Liga games until losing to Sevilla and then 4-0 to Barcelona at the Bernabéu in mid-November. This result was embarrassing, and there were more red faces two weeks later at Real's disqualification from the Copa del Rey round of 32 before the second leg against Cadiz. Real had fielded an ineligible player – recently signed Denis Cheryshev – in the first leg.

Benitez was sacked by Pérez in early January, with the president citing that Rafa was unpopular with fans, the players were unhappy and so on. This dismissal took little account of Real's current third place in La Liga. That same day, the coach of Casillas, who happened to be one Zinedine Zidane, was promoted to head coach of the senior team. In this, Zidane, the unofficial on-pitch leader from 2001 until 2006, was following the paths laid down by such as Muñoz, Molowny, Di Stéfano and Del Bosque, all players of distinction and notable managers with Real Madrid.

In La Liga, the season ended with the three leading clubs – Atlético, Barca and Real – within three points of each other, above whom sat Real's neighbours, Atlético Madrid. However, they were doing fine in the Champions League. In the quarter-final, having recovered from a 2-0 defeat by Wolfsburg in Germany with a Ronaldo hat-trick at home, they inched past Manchester City in the semi-final, thanks to an own goal in a 1-0 aggregate win.

Their opponents in the 2016 Champions League final, on 28 May in the San Siro, were again Atlético Madrid. Real's unrelenting centre-back and captain Sergio Ramos scored in the 15th minute from a blatantly offside position. Real then dominated the game, although a Griezmann penalty hit the crossbar, but they could not find a way through the carefully drilled Atlético defence. On a counter-attack, Atlético's Carrasco levelled from a Juanfran cross with 15 minutes remaining.

After a goalless extra time came penalties. With the score at three each, Juanfran hit the post while Ramos slotted home his effort. It was now down to Ronaldo (who else?), whose attempt hit the back of the net for Real's 11th European Cup. After the game, Ronaldo stated he had had 'a vision' that he would score the winner.

Diego Simeone, a realist by upbringing and experience, simply remarked, 'Real Madrid were better than us again.'

Who needs badges?

After he had retired from his supremely self-confident on-pitch activities, Zidane continued his management career with Real in a similar manner. He knew how to win football matches, and he had little need of coaching certificates to achieve this.

His first complete season at Real – 2016/17 – was one of the most successful in the club's history. Although Celta Vigo narrowly defeated his team 4-3 in the Copa quarter-final (that's that out of the way, then), by mid-September, Real's 16 straight wins was a club record. In early January, Benzema's last-minute goal in the 3-3 draw with Sevilla marked Real's establishment of another record: the first club in Spanish national football to reach 40 games without a loss. Real won La Liga.

Winning the Champions League had long since eclipsed El Clásico as the main indicator of Real's season, and Zizou had already beaten Napoli (6-2), Bayern Munich (6-3) and, in the semi-final first leg at the Bernabéu, Ronaldo's hat-trick had virtually rendered unnecessary the second leg in Real's 4-2 aggregate win over Atlético Madrid.

In the final against Juventus on 3 June 2017 at Cardiff's Millennium Stadium, Mandžukić's stylish overhead goal equalled Ronaldo's earlier strike, but the second half saw a dominant Real score three more for a 4-1 victory. Real Madrid had won their 12th European Cup, become the first club to retain the title in the Champions League era, and won La Liga and the Champions League in the same season, the first Real side to do so.

As one would expect, Zidane restricted himself to the terse comment that 'We are a very good side and we deserved to win La Liga and the Champions League.' Although the season which followed (2017/18) was not quite so remarkable – Real were third in La Liga and lost to Leganés in the quarter-final of the Copa – they again distinguished themselves in Europe. Ronaldo, with 44 goals, continued as the top scorer, but Pepe, James Rodriguez and Morata all left the club. Nevertheless, Real squeezed through to the final, beating PSG 4-3, Juventus 4-3 and Bayern Munich 4-3.

The quarter-final against Juventus was something of a sensation. Real won 3-0 in Turin, then after 60 minutes at the Bernabéu, the Italian side had unexpectedly drawn level. In injury time, a penalty was awarded in Real's favour, provoking a hysterical reaction from the Juventus players. Juventus keeper Buffon, celebrating his 650th appearance for the club, was sent off for fierce and repeated arguments, and was replaced. Seven minutes elapsed before Ronaldo finally took the penalty, and he sent his shot smacking into the right-hand corner of deputy Szczesny's net for the winning goal. Two minutes later, the final whistle blew.

At the Olympic Stadium in Kiev on 26 May 2018, Liverpool were the other finalists. Halfway through the first period, Ramos badly bodychecked Liverpool's Salah who shortly after had to retire, due to what seemed a deliberate foul. The referee did nothing. Benzema and Sané both scored after the interval: 1-1.

In the 60th minute, Bale replaced Isco, and three minutes later the Welshman sent a beautifully judged bicycle-kick into the Liverpool net. With seven minutes left, Bale sent in a speculative ball from 40 yards, the keeper made a disastrous misjudgement, and the score was 3-1 at the end. This was Real's 13th title, their third in succession. The losing keeper Karius received death threats and hate mail. By the start of the following season, he had been transferred to Besiktas.

Five days after his three-in-a-row victory, Zidane announced he was stepping down as Real needed a new manager with a 'different voice'. It's safe to assume that this complex man wasn't pushed, as he was back in the manager's chair before the next season ended.

Gareth Bale scores a wonder goal against Liverpool in the 2018 European Cup final. *Alamy*

Welcome back, Zizou

One of the more intriguing aspects of the game of football is the speed with which fortunes change. This observation is by way of introducing Real's season 2018/19 which, unlike its illustrious predecessor, was something of a failure, at least in terms of Real's expectations.

Two managers, each of whom lasted around four months, were followed by the return of Zidane, who had insufficient time to turn the season round. Julien Lopetegui and Santiago Solari were both fired, after the former lost 5-1 away to Barcelona in October and the latter lost 4-1 to Ajax at the Bernabéu in March. The *deus ex machina* was lowered to solve the problem.

Their positions at Real had not been helped by the departure of Ronaldo to Juventus in the summer of 2018. More of an institution than a player, Ronaldo had made 438 competitive appearances and scored 451 goals in his nine seasons at the club, according to the club's official website. Juventus paid around £100 million for the services of the 33-year-old superstar. However, Real did invest in the future with the acquisition from Flamengo of 18-year-old Vinícius Júnior, a winger with exciting potential.

In La Liga, Real were in third place at the season's end, 19 points behind winners Barcelona, while the Catalan side knocked them out 4-1 at the Copa semi-final stage in February.

Even Real's normal barnstorming finale, the Champions League, was a serious disappointment, at least for Madridismos, when they crashed out of the tournament at the hands of Ajax in the round of 32.

On 13 February, Real were fortunate to escape the Amsterdam Arena with a 2-1, first-leg lead over an inspired Ajax side who generally overwhelmed the European champions and deserved to win. 'We'll stuff them at the Bernabéu' must have been Ramos's reasoning behind his ensuring a deliberate yellow card in the last minute of the game, which meant that he'd miss the second leg and then have a clean sheet for the quarter-final onward.

It would have been interesting to sit next to Ramos at the Bernabéu on the evening of 5 March as a brilliant Ajax performance swept aside the Spanish 'masters'. The Dutch team overwhelmed Ramos's side, winning 4-1 and kicking an arrogantly complacent Real out of the competition. Unfortunately for neutrals and lovers of the game, Ajax were eliminated in the semi-finals. They had been a joy to watch.

Coping with Covid

This euphoria, however, was short-lived, as the two seasons which followed were badly disrupted by the Covid-19 pandemic. La Liga was suspended indefinitely on 23 March 2020 and resumed on 11 June but, until further notice, all games were to be played behind closed doors. Also, until the beginning of season 2021/22, Real's home ground became the 6,000-capacity Alfredo Di Stéfano Stadium at their training ground.

When the season eventually ended on 19 July, Real were champions with 87 points, five points ahead of second-placed Barcelona, although back in February they had been defeated 4-3 in the Copa quarter-final by Real Sociedad. Also, in the opening game of the Champions League knockout stage, Real had suffered a 2-1 home defeat by Manchester City, Isco scoring for Real. A full six months later, this scoreline was repeated in the second away leg, and Real were eliminated 4-2 on aggregate.

During the next season and still playing home fixtures at the Di Stéfano ground, Real won no trophies, their worst campaign since 2010/11. Although they were second in La Liga and reached the semi-final of the Champions League – where they were knocked out 3-1 by Chelsea – they succumbed to a Segunda B club in the Copa del Rey, remarkably for the fifth time in 20 years.

Alcoyano, from the small town of Alcoi, met Real in the round of 32 at their home ground in the Valencian Community on 21

January 2021. With the score 1-1 in extra time, and having had a defender sent off, Alcoyano scored within the last five minutes for a famous victory. The humiliated Real had few excuses, as their team contained Benzema, Marcelo, Cassemiro, Kroos and Eden Hazard, the last being an attacking midfielder bought the previous year for £100 million from Chelsea.

Naturally, Zidane was blamed for the debacle. *AS* damned the manager, saying 'Zidane's flower has wilted forever' and *Marca* commented, 'if he is saved from this it is a miracle'. Zidane assumed full responsibility: 'Whatever has to happen will happen.' What happened was that Zidane left the club in the summer, and Carlo Ancelotti was again appointed manager back at the Bernabéu as season 2021/22 kicked off.

Finale

In early June 2021, Carlo Ancelotti, then managing Everton, was again appointed first-team coach in the wake of Zidane's departure. Ancelotti was regarded as probably the finest manager in European football, having won league titles with the leading Continental clubs in Italy (AC Milan, 2004), England (Chelsea, 2010), France (Paris Saint-Germain, 2013) and Germany (Bayern Munich, 2017), as well as a host of other titles and honours. He was the most likely man to re-secure La Liga for Real.

Although the long-serving centre-back duo of Sergio Ramos and Raphael Varane left Real that summer – to join Paris Saint-Germain and Manchester United respectively – and the young Norwegian midfielder Martin Ødegaard had accepted an offer from Arsenal, there were several other newcomers. Notably, these included all-rounder but principally defender David Alaba from Bayern Munich and young midfield prodigy Eduardo Camavinga from Rennes. Also, on 12 September, Real enjoyed their first full-capacity game at home in the Bernabéu (despite the crowd limitations caused by the continuing renovation work) for over 560 days when they hosted Celta Vigo with a 5-2 defeat.

Indeed, that season they lost only three Liga games, all away, to Espanyol (October), Getafe (January) and, in March, a revitalised Barcelona who beat them 4-0. The canny presence of Ancelotti ensured that, after their 4-0 defeat of Espanyol on 30 April 2022, Real were uncatchable in La Liga with 81 points and four games in hand. The other contenders – Sevilla, Atlético Madrid and Barcelona – were simply too far away, and Real claimed their 35th Liga that day. Ironically, on 8 May, they were defeated 1-0 by Atlético at the Wanda Metropolitano, their only defeat at their neighbour's ground, but no matter. In just under three weeks, Real would again contest the Champions League final.

In the Champions League, UEFA had announced in June 2021 the abolition of the long-standing 'away goals rule' in all UEFA club competitions. In future, in the event of a draw over two games, the greater number of goals scored in the away match would no longer count as an automatic pass into the following round. Clubs now had to win two-match ties on goals alone.

On 15 February, Real had advanced to the tournament's 'round of 16' where they would meet Paris Saint-Germain, who boasted a forward line of Mbappé, Messi and Neymar, three of the world's most accomplished and exciting footballers. At a rainswept Parc des Princes, a goal from Mbappé in the 95th minute was sufficient for the French club to take a 1-0 lead to the Bernabéu. On 9 March, Mbappé scored again in the first half, but in the second period Karim Benzema's hat-trick within 17 blistering minutes, with assists from Modrić and Vinicius Junior, secured Real's passage, by an aggregate 3-2 win, to the quarter-final against Chelsea.

At Stamford Bridge on 6 April, Benzema scored his second successive hat-trick in Real's 3-1 win, while six days later at the Bernabéu, Chelsea were 3-0 ahead until Brazilian winger Rodrygo pulled one back for Real, courtesy of a defence-splitting, splendid through ball from 36-year-old Modrić. At the final whistle, with the score 4-4, the game entered extra

Karim Benzema completes his hat-trick at Stamford Bridge. *Colorsport*

time, when the equally ageing but consistently prolific Benzema (again) scored in the 96th minute. Real emerged with a much-deserved 5-4 victory and a semi-final against Pep Guardiola's Manchester City.

The first confrontation took place in Manchester on 26 April, just a few days before Real confirmed their unassailable dominance in that season's Liga but a full month before City, on the final day of the English season, did the same in England. So, the champions of Spain and England met again, and, just as in the quarter-final, it was an enthralling and ultimately spectacular two-match tie. It also revealed once more Real's ability to haul victory from the near certainty of defeat.

Two goals ahead after ten minutes at home, City were jubilant, but they had to be content with winning 4-3 when Benzema (yet again) replied with a couple and Vinicius added a third with a dummy and then an outstanding solo run from the halfway line. It was an even more closely contested match, with an astonishing conclusion, six days later in Madrid. At almost the end of 90 minutes of normal time, City were 5-3 ahead on aggregate and appeared to be cruising to the final. However, this all changed when substitute Rodrygo scored twice in two minutes in injury time. The game, now poised at 5-5, entered extra time, and who else but Benzema added another Real goal from the penalty spot. Real held on, finished 6-5 ahead over the two games, and had again reached the final of the Champions League.

The 'old boys' of Madrid, as they were increasingly being hailed, had done it again. In particular, Benzema – with his tireless on-pitch contribution and his season's tally of 44 goals – had replaced Ronaldo as the Bernabéu fans' 'favourite'. Vinicius, although still a youngster by the overall standards of the team, had been an outrageously gifted winger and supplier to Benzema.

INNERS

CHAMPIONS LEAGUE 2021/2022

Kroos, Casemiro and Modrić, as well as the gifted newcomer Camavinga, had adroitly controlled midfield throughout the season. And all the other team members had well supported the new manager. However, the ultimate test was awaiting them. They were to meet Liverpool in the final of the Champions League at the Stade de France on 28 May.

The final, the highlight of the season for European club football, had been scheduled to take place in St Petersburg, but the venue was hastily changed by UEFA after Russian Vladimir Putin's incursion into Ukraine. So, Paris it became. Four years previously, the two teams had met (ironically, in Ukraine) in the final, and Real's 3-1 victory was their third Champions League title in a row. Jurgen Klopp's Liverpool had just failed to win the English Premier League title, although they were otherwise riding high, and their style of play – as a coherent, pressing and powerful attacking side – made them slight favourites over Real's unpredictable but frequently brilliant movement on the pitch. It promised to be an exciting match, and a high-scoring one.

Finale: Courtois magnificent as Real claim 14th trophy

However, as we know, football is an unpredictable game, and even more so when Real are involved. The 2022 Champions League final was neither enthralling nor a goal-fest, and, at the final whistle, only one goal had been scored.

To add to the frustration, the match finally kicked off over 30 minutes later than advertised, due to a combination of inefficient planning by UEFA and the French riot police's unnecessary recourse to spraying pepper and tear gas over hundreds of queuing Liverpool fans. The delay was not helped by the extended song-and-dance act which UEFA found necessary to inflict on the increasingly impatient supporters of both teams.

The first half was largely dominated by Liverpool, who launched an extended attack on the Real defence, even though Benzema in the 43rd minute forced into the net a 'goal' which was disallowed by VAR. In the second period, however, Real began to press Liverpool and, in the 58th minute, launched a rare counter-attack. The energetic right-winger Valverde crossed to an unmarked Vinicius who tapped the ball into the Liverpool net for the winning goal, to the delight of the Madridismos crammed into the stand behind the goal. This was the moment when Liverpool's efforts seemed to fade away, as their players began to recognise the speedy thinking and durability of the

The 2021/22 La Liga champions. *Alamy*

Spanish club. Real refused to capitulate. The Scouse side's deflation was assisted by the growth in confidence of Real's midfield, especially Casemiro and Modrić, and the defence, with Carvajal and Mendy continually breaking up Liverpool's increasingly limp efforts to find an equaliser.

However, the one man responsible for Real's victory was without doubt the club's ex-Chelsea keeper Thibaut Courtois, whose goaltending was remarkable and at times breathtaking in its vision and execution. Indeed, the following morning's *Observer* rated his performance at a maximum ten points and awarded him the 'Man of the Match'. Few would disagree with this assessment of his critical role in the game.

Real had won their 14th European Cup/Champions League title, double the number achieved by the next most successful club AC Milan. Manager Ancelotti had secured five titles with different clubs, itself a significant record. Although several of their older players will no doubt be considering retirement, particularly after having endured such an heroic but exhausting campaign, there is at the Bernabéu no lack of equally effective but significantly younger players willing to take their places.

As has happened throughout their history, Real Madrid will continue as one of the greatest clubs in world football.

POLARIS
PUBLISHING